The Complete Book of Sauces

The Complete Book of Sauces

SALLIE Y. WILLIAMS

Produced by The Philip Lief Group, Inc. and Blackbirch Graphics, Inc.

MACMILLAN PUBLISHING COMPANY *New York*

COLLIER MACMILLAN PUBLISHERS *London*

Macmillan Publishing Company
866 Third Avenue, New York, N.Y. 10022
Collier Macmillan Canada, Inc.

Produced by The Philip Lief Group, Inc.

Library of Congress Cataloging-in-Publication Data

Williams, Sallie Y.
    The complete book of sauces / Sallie Y. Williams; produced by the
Philip Lief Group, Inc.
        p.   cm.
    ISBN 0-02-629391-9
    1. Sauces.   2. Salad dressings.   I. Philip Lief Group.
    II. Title.
    TX819.A1W55   1990
641.8'14—dc20   89-14008   CIP

Printed in the United States of America

❧ *Contents*

❧ *Acknowledgments*

THIS SAUCE BOOK WAS THE INSPIRATION OF RICHARD AND BRUCE Glassman, who also made its publication possible. Their faith in me has been an enormous support, and I hope their inspiration has become a satisfying reality.

I am especially indebted to Nancy Kalish for her eternal enthusiasm and untiring effort to make this book the best it could be—and to Philip Lief for being such a supporter.

My thanks also to my family, who continue to submit themselves to wave after wave of testing and tasting, and who offer constructive suggestions from time to time, occasionally along with more colorful comments.

CHAPTER ONE

❧ *Setting Up for Saucemaking*

IN THIS MODERN AGE OF WEIGHT-WATCHING AND HEALTH CONSCIOUSNESS, when fads come and go with enough rapidity to make your head spin, why are we even considering a collection of sauces?

Sauces are nearly as old as cooking. While they have been created for varying reasons over the centuries, the result has generally been a concoction that was added toward the end of cooking, or after the main ingredient had been fully prepared. Today saucemaking is in a period of rapid change. Classic sauces seem to have gone out of favor and have been replaced by more "natural" preparations that do not contain much salt, fat, or thickeners. But while this would appear to be the case in restaurants, the sauce, including the most classic varieties, is alive and well in the home. The time has come for a collection of recipes that offers the home cook many of the classic, as well as the more modern, innovative combinations. It is also time to encourage enthusiastic cooks to try their hand at creating their own, personal variations of more traditional preparations.

In order to understand what is happening in this realm of the culinary world, it is first essential to decide just what constitutes a sauce. Today the answer is often difficult to discern. Is it something that simply amplifies or complements the flavors of the main ingredient of a dish? Or is a sauce something that adds its own flavors, thereby creating a final taste that is entirely different from either element alone?

In fact, a sauce can be any of these things. And each type has a definite place in cooking. It would be a shame to lose the flexibility of all kinds of combinations by becoming locked into thinking of sauces as only simple reductions of cooking juices, a spoonful of olive oil, or a few chopped vegetables.

Generally, a sauce is any liquid that accompanies a dish. It usually adds flavor, sometimes texture, and frequently color to the final recipe. Often the liquid is thickened in some way. Julia Child, who sees cooking with very clear vision, says, "Sauce is an accompaniment, either to moisten the food it goes with or to contrast in taste. It is not a disguise. It is an embellishment. It has nothing to do with health. It can be simple or rich. It can be anything you want it to be."

As she so clearly points out, that is the essence of a sauce—it is anything you want it to be. It can be something carefully prepared over long hours and through many steps, or it can be something thrown together at the last minute with whatever is on hand. The only thing to keep in mind is that a sauce is indeed "an embellishment," something that *partners* the food it is accompanying. It should not be the dominant taste.

This has not been the case throughout history. Ancient sauces were very strong, dominating flavors that often hid inferior or spoiled meats or other foods. In fact, early sauces were probably more like ketchup and mustard than they were sauces as we think of them today. While sauces were certainly in use before Roman times, our first real knowledge of them comes from the cookery manuscripts of Apicius. These "recipes" were for combinations that included the fermented fish paste *liquamen* (which must have been very much like the Oriental fish sauce *nuoc mam*—a little fishy and very salty); *verjus* (the juice of sour or unripe grapes), much pepper, and a varying quantity of other spices.

There was another category of sauce in ancient times. When a society was rich enough to use salt, foods were preserved with it—very much in the manner of our salt cod and ham. No matter how long these foods were soaked before being used in a final dish, the overall flavor must have been—salt. To help counteract this overpowering saltiness, recipes were developed for very bland, pasty sauces, thickened for the most part with bread crumbs. While these would be very unappealing by themselves, they must have served their purpose admirably.

Later, by the sixteenth century, the Italians seem to have mastered the art of flour-thickened sauces which were much easier to produce consistently. The marriage of Catherine de Medici to Henri II of France in 1553 brought this art to France, where it was refined and, finally, about a century later, "standardized" by Pierre François de La Varenne. By the mid-eighteenth century certain combinations were becoming known by very precise names. Béchamel, still the standard white sauce today, was developed for Louis de Béchamel in the court of Louis XIV. Soubise, a white sauce with onions added, and Mornay, a white sauce flavored with cheese, were probably developed by chefs serving a French prince and a prominent Huguenot family. Hollandaise might have been created in Holland by Huguenots who had been forced to flee France—and so sauce history goes.

The French sauce "system" depended on certain very definite bases. Stock was the first essential element, whether it was made from chicken, beef, veal, or fish. Then came three or four base sauces, such as béchamel, velouté, espagnole, and tomato sauces. Variations on each of those base sauces then resulted in literally hundreds of subtly different preparations.

Italy seemed to forgo the flour-thickened sauces early on and, once the tomato was introduced and widely accepted, developed innumerable combinations of vegetables, oils, wines, and herbs that complemented rather than overwhelmed the foods with which they were served. Over time, cooks slightly thickened many of these sauces in order to better cling to pasta.

Recently, in the name of "lighter" eating, flour has been eliminated from many sauces, and recipes are often thickened with butter. That change has done little to remove calories or cholesterol, but it has created sauces that look and feel lighter. Recently, enterprising chefs have concentrated on preparations that are thickened by reducing a liquid to its flavorful essence or by adding a thick puree of vegetables. These sauces do tend to be less caloric, less time-consuming, and often emphasize, rather than alter, the flavor of the central ingredient. Coarse vinaigrettes, olive oil, herbs, and finely minced vegetables such as onions, peppers, and tomatoes are sometimes now the only accompaniments to the meat or fish being served. And, incidentally, portion size has definitely diminished as well.

The modern saucemaker is no longer confined to the recipes of one geographic region. Sauces and condiments from Europe are joined by preparations from the Orient, the Middle East, North Africa, South America, and Mexico, to name just a few. There is no reason to fall into the rut of serving only a handful of old standbys when there are hundreds of wonderful flavor combinations to experiment with.

The reason that sauces are still with us is that they enhance, complement, and sometimes alter the flavors of the foods we serve. This collection of recipes should provide many wonderful eating experiences, especially since most of the sauces herein can be served with a variety of foods—thus increasing your repertoire exponentially with each new preparation you master.

❧ MASTERING THE ART OF SAUCEMAKING

If there is one key to successful saucemaking, it is practice. In France, apprentices spend years learning to create the same sauces day after day so that the customer will never be disappointed. Beginning with the preparation of vegetables and bones for the *fonds* (foundations or stocks, as we call them), an apprentice then moves on to making the stocks themselves. When he has mastered these, after some time, he begins making the basic sauces from which all the others are derived. In many hard-knock kitchens, it's not uncommon for the *Saucier,* or Sauce Chef, to taste the results of an entire morning's efforts, pronounce them unfit and insist the sauces be made again—from scratch.

While most of these complicated sauces are no longer popular, it is a good idea to learn how to make them. By doing so, a cook can follow the progression of a sauce from the moment water is added to bones to make a stock to the final complex preparations that are still appropriate on many occasions. Understanding the stages of complex saucemaking will help facilitate making even the most rudimentary reduction of pan juices.

Practice also helps you understand how sauces behave—how not to be afraid of a hollandaise, how to avoid overly hot temperatures when making an emulsified butter sauce, how to sense when the quantity of fat has become too much for the liquid available (which will cause the sauce to separate), how to reduce liquids without burning them, and many other techniques that will make you a Master Sauce Maker.

ADVANCE PREPARATION

The second most important element in saucemaking—as in any kind of cooking—is advance preparation. It is absolutely essential to read the recipe thoroughly beforehand, understanding exactly what the ingredients are, how they are prepared before cooking begins, and what techniques will be employed in making the sauce. Check and be sure that you have all the ingredients and equipment you will need and then place them within arm's reach.

Once all the necessary raw ingredients and equipment are assembled, the next step is to create the *mise en place,* or literally, "the putting in place." Everything needed should be measured, peeled, cut up, softened, chilled, or had done to it whatever is called for in the instructions. All this should be done before any cooking or assembling of the sauce is begun. Much of it can be done well in advance so that the final preparation is short and quick.

The recipes in this collection have been designed to help you make an effective *mise en place*. As much as possible, preliminary preparation has been indicated right beside the ingredient in the listing at the beginning of the recipe. All you have to do is follow the list, from top to bottom, one ingredient at a time, until all are ready to be made into the sauce. Arrange the prepared ingredients in order on a large tray or on your counter. They will be incorporated into the recipe in the order in which they appear in the listing.

✿ UNDERSTANDING SAUCES

Now that most of the work is done, it is time to understand a little about sauces themselves. Details about specific types of sauces will be found in the individual chapter introductions, but there are many hints that apply to almost all the recipes.

THICKENING

A sauce can be thickened in many ways. Once you are comfortable with many of the recipes in this book, you can work on your own combinations, using the basic method of thickening you prefer. You can thicken sauces with flour, cornstarch, arrowroot, potato starch, kneaded butter, emulsified butter, vegetable purees, reduced liquids, egg yolks, and cream. Some thickeners are fast acting, some require longer cooking—and some are very tricky.

Whenever *egg yolks* are added to a finished sauce, it may be heated thoroughly, but must never be boiled again. Too high a temperature will coagulate the egg, curdling the sauce. Once an egg-finished sauce has curdled, nothing can be done to make it smooth again. When adding egg yolks to any hot liquid, it is important to beat a small amount of the hot liquid into the eggs before beating them into the remaining liquid. This cooks the egg a little, warms it up, and tends to dilute the egg yolk so that it will not curdle on contact with the mass of hot sauce.

Beating is the key word here; the quicker the egg is incorporated into the hot liquid, the less chance it will curdle. A flexible wire whisk is the perfect tool. For an ultrasmooth sauce, strain the finished preparation through a fine sieve. Some chefs spoon the sauce through a small sieve as they prepare each plate serving.

Cornstarch, arrowroot, and *potato starch* are last-minute thickeners which have twice the thickening power of flour. These should not be cooked for more than a few minutes after they have been added or the sauce will become thin again. These thickeners provide a translucent, glossy finish. Many Oriental sauces make use of the quick thickening power of cornstarch or arrowroot.

Kneaded butter is a good emergency thickener—or for those moments when you decide on the spur of the moment to create a sauce out of the liquid left in the cooking pan. Equal amounts of butter and flour are mixed together to form a thick paste. Bits of this paste are beaten into the sauce with a whisk until it reaches the desired degree of thickness. Combining the flour with a fat prevents it from forming lumps when it touches a hot liquid, and, in addition, the butter tends to give a shine to the finished sauce. Once the kneaded butter has thickened the sauce, it should not be reboiled, as it tends to separate under high heat.

If calories are not important, *heavy cream* will thicken a sauce when it is boiled to reduce the liquid in it. If a cream sauce becomes over-cooked, but not burned, and has separated or appears very oily, stir a little water, wine, or stock into it and beat with a whisk.

FLAVORINGS

Many flavorings can be added early in the saucemaking process. Wine, herbs, pepper, and other spices will add more flavor with long cooking. Salt, however, should be added near the end of the cooking time. As the cooking progresses, the liquid is reduced and salt will become increasingly concentrated. It is much easier to add more salt at the end than to try to overcome a too salty taste. The one time when it is necessary to be generous with salt is in the preparation of a cooked sauce that will be served cool or chilled. Chilling tends to reduce flavor and all seasonings should be accentuated.

It is important to remember that saucing is just as important today as it has been in the past. Even if a sauce adds little except eye appeal, it can be the difference between a good dish and a great dish. At the health and weight loss spas that are so popular these days, the chefs continue to search for ways to add that little extra burst of flavor—without the extra calories. And often that is accomplished through the sauce, even if it is simply a spoonful of extra-virgin olive oil.

With this book always at hand in the kitchen, there should never be a single occasion when you will not be able to enhance a dish with ingredients you already have on hand. The more stained, marked-up, and well-thumbed this volume becomes, the more proficient you will become in the art of saucemaking.

❈SAUCEMAKING EQUIPMENT

Most of the tools for saucemaking are probably right in your kitchen at this moment. It is not essential to run out and buy expensive equipment in order to become a competent maker of sauces. There are, however, several items that might be very nice to have.

1 large *(6 quart or larger)* stockpot—heavy-gauge aluminum or Calphelon

3 saucepans *(1 quart, 1½ quarts, and 2 quarts)*—heavy-gauge aluminum with separate construction handles; stainless steel over copper; copper with a stainless steel or nickel lining; Calphelon (but not for use with acidic sauces, as the pans will discolor the sauce); or enamel over steel. (The very best beurre blanc I ever ate was in a little restaurant in Paris where the woman chef used only the old-fashioned enamel pots that can be bought very cheaply.)

2 whisks *(1 small, one medium size)*—tinned steel or stainless steel, somewhat rigid, with either metal or wooden handles

wooden spoons in a variety of shapes and sizes

sieves—1 chinois *(or Chinese cap)* for straining stocks and large quantities of sauces (it is almost as effective as cheesecloth), and one small and one medium-size conical strainer for straining small quantities of sauce

blender—handy for making quick emulsified sauces

food processor—a must for making purees and very smooth sauces

knives—sharp, well-balanced, and of stainless steel, in various sizes

grater—stainless steel box type, if you prefer grating by hand

measuring spoons—1 set of good quality

liquid measures—one- and two-cup, of glass, if possible

mixing bowls in assorted sizes

CHAPTER TWO

❧ *Stocks and Stock-based Sauces*

STOCKS, OR *fonds* AS THEY ARE CALLED IN FRANCE, ARE THE BASES OF MANY traditional sauces. While making them is a time-consuming process, they freeze admirably well and are ready almost instantly for future use.

There are four basic stocks: Brown stock, made with beef and bones that are grilled to give the final product a rich brown color; veal or white stock, made with veal bones, which produce a very gelatinous, almost clear liquid that will not mask the flavors of sauces made with it; chicken stock, also a rich, clear liquid with a pronounced chicken flavor; and fish stock or *fumet,* a quickly made base for sauces to be used with fish and shellfish.

In addition, there is *court bouillon,* literally a short stock made in ten minutes, which is generally prepared as a poaching liquid and takes on the flavor of the fish that is cooked in it. If a sauce is made from the poaching liquid, it simply adds a more pronounced flavor to the fish it is served with.

Traditionally, stocks are cooked on the back of the stove for hours. While many modern chefs have reduced this cooking time, the final product is not nearly as full flavored as stocks prepared the old-fashioned way. Once the initial preparations are made, the bones browned, vegetables cleaned, etc., the stock itself can simmer (but never boil) unattended for hours. Even eight to ten hours is not too long for a stock to cook. Remember that it should absorb all the flavors from the meats and vegetables it is prepared with. Once the stock is strained and simmered again to concentrate the flavors even further, it can be ladled into containers and frozen. Consequently, stockmaking can be an occasional rainy weekend project that requires very little attention.

STOCK TIPS

- Don't use any salt in a stock. As the liquid reduces, salt would become very concentrated; it should be added only when the final sauce is being prepared.

- Use a heavyweight stockpot—aluminum is easiest to lift when full—that is deep with straight sides. The stockpot should fit comfortably on a large burner.

- Stocks are best when simmered uncovered.

- A well-made stock should contain a great deal of gelatin derived from the bones used, especially when they're veal bones. If a stock is refrigerated rather than frozen, it should gel completely when cooled, and can be spooned, as is, directly into a saucepan for further use.

- If stocks are to be used frequently over a period of a week, they can be refrigerated, but should be taken out of the refrigerator every two to three days, boiled for 10 minutes in an open saucepan, and rerefrigerated in a clean container. This will eliminate any possibility of bacteria developing in the liquid. The same rule applies to any sauces made with stocks. But since boiling a finished sauce is likely to destroy it, it's best to plan never to store a stock-based sauce for more than two or three days.

- Brown stock can be reduced until it is dark and almost the consistency of syrup. Once cooled, this essence is somewhat like rubber, but is really the ancient equivalent of a modern bouillon cube. Only a tablespoon or two of this meat glaze is needed to flavor several cups of sauce, and it keeps for months in the refrigerator.

- Simmering bones for stock will cause a foam (made of albumin and impurities) to form on the surface of the stock. Skimming off this foam is an important step in stockmaking. This step is only necessary in the beginning when first bringing all the ingredients to a boil. Careful skimming produces a clear stock that is not the least bit bitter.

- Once the stock is strained, it can be refrigerated for several hours. Any fat will rise to the surface and solidify when cool. This can simply be removed with a spoon and discarded. The nearly fat-free final product can then be used, refrigerated, or frozen.

- Some purists add wine only to fish stock, but I think the flavor of any stock is enhanced with a cup or two of hearty wine. Use red wine for brown stock, white wine for veal, chicken, or fish stock.

- When a bouquet garni is called for, prepare one by tying together several sprigs of fresh thyme, a bay leaf, and some thick stems of parsley. This should be removed when the stock is strained.

- While any of the recipes in this book that require stock can be made with commercial broths or bouillon cubes, the end result will be decidedly saltier than those made from home-made stock. It is a good idea to take this into consideration when seasoning the final sauce made with storebought stock.

❧ COURT BOUILLON

Court bouillon is really a short stock. The liquid and the vegetables in it are used to poach fish and will cook a second time. A short first simmer gives a more flavorful cooking liquid.

> 2 cups dry white wine
> 1 stalk celery, chopped
> 1 large onion, chopped
> 1 large carrot, scrubbed (not peeled) and chopped
> 1 bay leaf
> 8 to 10 whole black peppercorns
> Salt to taste
> 2 cups water

In a large saucepan over low heat, simmer all the ingredients for 10 minutes.

YIELD: ABOUT 4 CUPS

❦ BROWN STOCK

It is not difficult to make stock at home, and the results are well worth the trouble. Far healthier and tastier than any kind of commercial stock base, homemade stock produces sauces of infinitely higher quality as well. Don't hurry the process; most stocks benefit from long, slow simmering on the back of the stove.

> 2 *pounds beef bones and trimmings*
> 2 *pounds veal bones, cut up*
> 3 *large carrots, scrubbed (not peeled) and cut up*
> 3 *large onions, quartered*
> 1 *stalk celery, split*
> 1 *clove garlic, crushed*
> 2 *tablespoons olive oil*
> 2 *cups dry, hearty red wine*
> 1 *bunch fresh parsley*
> *Several sprigs fresh thyme*
> *Freshly ground black pepper to taste*
> 8 *cups water*

Preheat the oven to 400°F. Spread the bones, carrots, onions, celery, and garlic in a roasting pan and sprinkle them with the oil. Roast, turning the bones from time to time, until very well browned, about 1½ hours. Scrape the bones and vegetables into a large stock kettle. Add the remaining ingredients and simmer over low heat for 4 to 5 hours, or longer, skimming the foam from the surface from time to time. Then strain the stock through a chinois and allow it to cool. Skim off any fat and chill.

YIELD: ABOUT 6 CUPS

❧ CHICKEN STOCK

Not only does homemade chicken stock make an excellent base for many sauces, it is the perfect beginning for soups of all kinds. Nothing tempts lazy appetites like a bowl of homemade chicken and vegetable soup.

> 5 pounds chicken necks, backs, and wings
> 1 cup dry white wine
> 8 cups water
> 2 teaspoons salt
> 2 large carrots, scrubbed (not peeled) and chopped
> 2 stalks celery, chopped
> 2 large whole leeks, well washed and halved
> 1 clove garlic, crushed
> Small bunch fresh parsley
> 10 whole black peppercorns

In a heavy kettle, combine the backs, necks, wings, wine, and water and simmer over low heat for 30 minutes. Skim well. Add the remaining ingredients and simmer 2 to 3 hours longer. Cool, skim off any fat, and strain through a chinois. Add salt to taste.

YIELD: ABOUT 8 CUPS

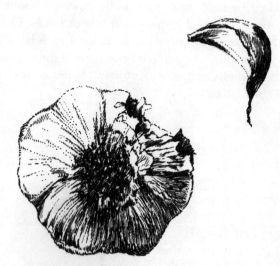

❧ FISH STOCK

Fish stock is simmered longer than court bouillon, but rarely for more than 20 minutes. Most chefs feel that a longer cooking time makes the stock bitter.

> 2 pounds fish heads and bones
> 1 cup dry white wine
> 1 large onion, sliced
> 1 large carrot, scrubbed (not peeled) and sliced
> 1 bouquet garni
> Salt to taste
> 5 cups water

Place all the ingredients in a large, heavy kettle and simmer over low heat for 20 minutes, skimming if you wish. Strain through a chinois.

YIELD: ABOUT 5 CUPS

❧ WHITE OR VEAL STOCK

White stock is generally used as a base for delicately flavored sauces. This stock adds little or no color to the final sauce.

> 5 pounds veal bones, cut up
> 10 cups cold water
> 2 large onions, quartered
> 3 large carrots, scrubbed (not peeled) and cut up
> 1 stalk celery, split
> 3 large whole leeks, well washed and split
> Several sprigs fresh thyme
> Several sprigs fresh parsley
> 10 whole black peppercorns

Place the bones and water in a large stock kettle. Bring to a boil and skim well. Add the remaining ingredients, turn heat down to low, and simmer for 3½ to 4 hours. Strain through a chinois and allow to cool; then skim off the fat and chill. The cold stock will be quite gelatinous.

YIELD: ABOUT 6 CUPS

❧ AVGOLEMONO (GREEK EGG AND LEMON SAUCE)

Avgolemono is easy to make and creates quite a stir at a formal dinner party. It is an almost ethereal sauce, light, foamy, and a beautiful pale yellow color. It is a great accompaniment to roasted meat or chicken, or poached fish, and I recommend it heartily for boiled artichokes. Add another cup of chicken stock and serve this as a perfect first course soup.

> *3 large eggs*
> *Juice of 1 lemon (about ¼ cup)*
> *1½ cups well-seasoned Chicken Stock (page 12), simmering*

In a large mixing bowl, beat the eggs with a whisk until lemon colored and frothy, then beat in the lemon juice until the mixture is very foamy. Whisk in the hot stock a little at a time until the sauce is light in color and foamy. Serve immediately.

YIELD: ABOUT 2 CUPS

❧ BASIL SAUCE

This easy sauce will make a celebration out of any baked or poached fish. Add it to your summer repertoire and use it to enhance charcoal-grilled salmon steaks, swordfish, and other firm-fleshed fish.

> *⅔ cup Fish Stock (page 13), boiled over high heat until reduced by one-quarter*
> *½ cup heavy cream*
> *2 tablespoons fresh lemon juice*
> *¼ cup heavy cream, whipped to stiff peaks*
> *¼ cup chopped fresh basil*
> *Salt and freshly ground black pepper to taste*

Combine the fish stock and cream in a heavy, medium-size saucepan. Reduce the liquid over medium heat by half, approximately 8 to 10 minutes. Stir in the lemon juice, then gently mix in the whipped cream and basil. Season and serve at once.

YIELD: ABOUT 1½ CUPS

❧ BASIC BROWN SAUCE

While this very basic sauce is excellent by itself over beef, noodles, and some game, such as venison and bear, it is generally used as a base for other, more complex sauces, several of which are included in this book. It may seem very time-consuming to make a brown stock, then this basic brown sauce, and then a finished sauce, but the result is well worth the effort. Both the stock and this sauce can be frozen for up to three months, which means you can make your own instant bases to have on reserve, which will speed up the process.

> 3 tablespoons butter
> 1 large carrot, scrubbed (not peeled) and chopped
> 1 stalk celery, chopped
> 2 large onions, chopped
> 1/4 cup flour
> 6 cups Brown Stock (page 11)
> 1 clove garlic, crushed
> 1 bouquet garni
> 1/3 cup tomato puree

Melt the butter in a heavy saucepan over medium heat. Add the carrot, celery, and onions and sauté until golden, taking care not to let them brown. All at once, stir in the flour, and turn the heat down to low. Cook, stirring occasionally, until the flour and vegetables are well browned, but not burned. Stir in the stock, then add the garlic, bouquet garni, and tomato puree. Simmer for 1 hour, stirring from time to time, or until the sauce is reduced by half. Strain. Allow to cool, then chill and skim off any fat before using.

YIELD: ABOUT 3 CUPS

❧ BIGARADE

Here is a classic sauce that is generally served with roast duck. Don't hesitate, however, to serve it with roast or grilled pork or ribs or with grilled chicken or turkey as well.

> 1 teaspoon cornstarch
> 1/3 cup orange juice
> 1 1/2 cups White or Veal Stock (page 13) or chicken broth
> 1 teaspoon sugar
> Zest of 1 orange, blanched for one minute in boiling water and drained
> 1 teaspoon dried thyme, or 1 tablespoon chopped fresh thyme
> Salt and freshly ground black pepper to taste
> 2 tablespoons Grand Marnier or other orange liqueur
> 1/2 cup fresh orange sections, seeded (optional)

Stir the cornstarch into the orange juice in a small bowl to make a smooth paste. Then stir the mixture into the stock. Pour into a heavy saucepan and add the sugar, zest, and thyme. Bring the sauce to a boil, then reduce the heat and simmer until it is clear and thickened, about 2 to 3 minutes. Season with salt and pepper and stir in the Grand Marnier. If desired, stir the orange sections into the very hot sauce just before serving. Serve immediately, and do not reboil.

YIELD: ABOUT 1 1/2 CUPS

❧ BONNE FEMME SAUCE

This "housewife's" sauce can be made at the last minute from ingredients that are almost always in the refrigerator. Even a plain piece of fish can become "company fare" when served with a Bonne Femme Sauce. Make it with chicken stock and serve it over poached eggs instead of hollandaise, or pour it over steamed vegetables.

> 2 large egg yolks
> 1/2 cup heavy cream, scalded (heated just until bubbles form around edges of pan)
> 2 cups Fish Stock (page 13), heated to boiling
> 2 tablespoons (1/4 stick) butter
> Salt and freshly ground white pepper to taste

Beat the egg yolks in a large mixing bowl until light, then whisk in the scalded cream. Next, pour the boiling stock into the egg mixture and beat in the butter. Season with salt and pepper and serve immediately.

YIELD: ABOUT 2 1/2 CUPS

❧ BORDELAISE SAUCE

Here is a rich, delicious sauce for special occasions. Serve it with grilled steak or roast beef for a really elegant dining experience. Ask your butcher for the marrow; its rich flavor is indispensable to the recipe. This sauce can be prepared up to two days in advance. Before serving, rewarm over low heat until very hot.

> 3 large shallots, minced
> 2/3 cup dry red wine
> Salt and freshly ground black pepper to taste
> 1 teaspoon chopped fresh thyme
> 4 tablespoons (1/2 stick) butter
> 1 tablespoon flour
> 1 cup Brown Stock (page 11), boiled over high heat until reduced to 2/3 cup
> 2 tablespoons beef marrow, cubed, poached 5 minutes in simmering water to cover, and drained
> 3 tablespoons chopped fresh parsley

Place the shallots, wine, salt, pepper, and thyme in a small saucepan and bring to a boil. Continue to boil until the liquid is reduced by one half. Remove from the heat and strain through a sieve.

Melt 1 tablespoon of the butter in a heavy saucepan over medium heat. Stir in the flour, turn down the heat to low, and cook until browned, about 2 minutes. Then pour in the stock and continue to simmer over low heat for another 15 to 20 minutes, stirring from time to time. Stir in the reduced wine and the marrow and cook several minutes longer. Remove from the heat, beat in the remaining butter and stir in the parsley. Check and correct seasonings, if necessary, and serve very hot.

YIELD: ABOUT 1 CUP

CLASSIC MUSHROOM SAUCE

Once you know how to make this sauce, you will want to put it on top of *everything*. Steak, roast beef, meat loaf, hamburgers, veal, chicken, turkey, pot roast, baked potatoes, egg noodles—the list goes on. The wine and the shallots especially bring out the flavors of meat and poultry. This sauce will keep in the refrigerator for up to two days. Rewarm over low heat before serving.

> 3 tablespoons butter
> 3 tablespoons flour
> 1¼ cups Brown Stock (page 11) or beef bouillon
> ¼ pound mushrooms, minced
> ¼ cup chopped shallots or scallions
> ¼ cup red wine
> Freshly ground black pepper to taste

Melt the butter in a small saucepan over medium heat. Remove it from the heat and whisk in the flour a little at a time until smooth. Return to low heat and, stirring constantly, cook until mixture turns golden brown, about 5 minutes.

Gradually add the stock, stirring until thickened, about 5 minutes. Pour in the mushrooms, shallots, and wine and combine. Heat through and add pepper to taste.

YIELD: ABOUT 2 CUPS

❦ COGNAC SAUCE

This sophisticated sauce will quickly become a favorite at your house. Spoon it over grilled veal chops or a crisp roast duck, and you will present a memorable dish indeed. It is outstanding over noodles for a small, but rich, first course.

> 2 tablespoons (¼ stick) butter
> 2 large shallots, minced
> 1 clove garlic, minced
> 2 tablespoons cognac
> ½ cup Brown Stock (page 11)
> ½ cup heavy cream
> 4 ounces shitake mushrooms, sliced
> Salt and freshly ground black pepper to taste

Melt the butter in a heavy medium-size saucepan over medium heat. Add the shallots and garlic and sauté until transparent, about 3 to 4 minutes. Then add the cognac and flame. To do this, remove the saucepan from the heat and touch a lighted match to the edge of the pan; the fumes of the cognac will ignite. Holding the pan away from you, allow the flames to die down naturally. Add the stock and cream and simmer over low heat until thickened, about 15 to 20 minutes. Add the mushrooms and continue to simmer 3 to 5 minutes more. Season with salt and pepper and serve immediately.

YIELD: ABOUT 1 CUP

❧ CREOLE SAUCE

There is a subtle Spanish influence in anything Creole, and this sauce is no exception. Not only is it perfect with all kinds of shellfish, but it will also enhance all but the most delicate fish. Spoon it over poached eggs or an omelet, or add a few cooked shrimp and pour over rice for a terrific supper dish. Prepare this sauce no more than one day in advance. Rewarm over low heat before serving.

> 2 tablespoons (1/4 stick) butter
> 1 medium-size green bell pepper, seeded and thinly sliced
> 1 medium-size onion, thinly sliced
> 1/2 cup thinly sliced fresh mushrooms
> 1 cup Brown Stock (page 11)
> 1 clove garlic, crushed
> 3 large, ripe tomatoes, peeled, seeded, and chopped
> Salt and freshly ground black pepper to taste
> Pinch of red (cayenne) pepper
> 1 tablespoon chopped fresh thyme or 1/2 teaspoon dried
> 2 tablespoons dry sherry

Melt the butter in a large, heavy saucepan over medium heat. Add the pepper and onion and sauté until transparent, about 4 or 5 minutes. Then add the mushrooms and sauté 5 minutes longer. Stir in the stock, garlic, and tomatoes. Season with salt, pepper, and thyme and simmer over low heat for 20 minutes. Stir in sherry and serve very hot.

YIELD: ABOUT 1 1/2 CUPS

❧ ESPAGNOLE SAUCE

The Spanish in this sauce comes from the addition of sherry. This aromatic brown sauce goes very well with roast beef, ham, or pork, and even tastes wonderful over baked potatoes. You can substitute Madeira for the sherry if you'd like a slightly sweeter sauce.

> *2 cups Basic Brown Sauce (page 15)*
> *2 tablespoons meat extract (such as Bovril)*
> *¼ cup dry sherry*

Place the brown sauce in a medium-size saucepan and reduce over low heat by one third, about 15 minutes or more. Stir in the extract and simmer an additional 15 minutes. Add the sherry and cook gently for 5 minutes longer. Serve immediately.

YIELD: ABOUT 2 CUPS

❧ HERB SAUCE

Just a little of this colorful sauce will turn any meat or poultry dish into something special. Try it on poached eggs, too, or as a sauce for pasta or rice.

> *3 tablespoons butter*
> *2 large shallots, finely chopped*
> *½ cup (2 ounces) finely chopped mushrooms*
> *2 tablespoons flour*
> *1 cup Chicken Stock (page 12)*
> *½ cup dry white wine*
> *1 tablespoon chopped fresh chives*
> *1 tablespoon chopped fresh tarragon*
> *3 tablespoons chopped fresh parsley*
> *Salt and freshly ground black pepper to taste*

Melt the butter in a large, heavy saucepan over medium heat. Stir in the shallots and mushrooms and sauté until tender, about 5 or 6 minutes. Whisk in the flour, then add the stock and stir until smooth. Simmer over low heat until the sauce is thick, about 5 minutes. Add the wine and herbs and simmer 5 to 10 minutes longer. Season to taste and serve immediately.

YIELD: ABOUT 1½ CUPS

❦ LYONNAISE SAUCE

Onions play a large part in the hearty cooking of the region around Lyon, France. This sauce incorporates the sweetness of fresh onions in a base of brown sauce, and is really an all-around accompaniment. Try it on eggs, over cooked vegetables, with cold roast meats, grilled chops— nearly anything that's full-flavored.

> 2 tablespoons (1/4 stick) butter
> 2 large onions, chopped
> 1/2 cup dry white wine
> 1 cup Basic Brown Sauce (page 15)
> 1 tablespoon chopped fresh parsley

Melt the butter in a medium-size, heavy saucepan over medium heat. Add the onions and sauté gently until golden, about 10 minutes. Stir in the wine and cook over high heat until liquid is reduced by half. Pour in the brown sauce and simmer over low heat for 15 minutes. Add the parsley, cook 1 minute longer, and serve immediately.

YIELD: ABOUT 2 CUPS

❦ ORANGE PORT SAUCE

A rich, unctuous mixture, this fruity sauce is the perfect way to make the most of a crisp roast duck or crackling roast loin of pork. If desired, this sauce can be prepared up to two days in advance and refrigerated. Rewarm over low heat before serving.

> 1/2 cup ruby port
> 1/2 cup Chicken Stock (page 12)
> 1/2 cup heavy cream
> 1 tablespoon chopped fresh rosemary
> 1/2 cup Seville (bitter) orange marmalade
> 1/4 cup dry white wine

Boil the port and stock in a medium-size saucepan over high heat until the liquid has been reduced by half, about 10 minutes. Stir in the cream and rosemary and boil over medium heat for another 5 minutes. Add the marmalade and stir until dissolved; then add the wine and cook for 5 more minutes over medium heat. Serve hot.

YIELD: ABOUT 1 CUP

❧ PEPPER SAUCE (POIVRADE)

This easy version of the classic pepper sauce clearly illustrates why some old-time combinations just cannot be improved upon. Serve this with beef or game, especially pheasant. This sauce will also keep for two days in the refrigerator. Rewarm over low heat before serving.

2 ounces slab bacon, diced
2 large onions, chopped
2 large carrots, peeled and chopped
3 large shallots, minced
1 large leek, white part only, well washed and thinly sliced
2 tablespoons red wine vinegar
2 tablespoons flour
1 clove garlic, crushed
2 cups Red Wine Marinade (page 112) or dry, hearty red wine
1 bouquet garni
2 cups Brown Stock (page 11)
1 tablespoon whole black peppercorns, crushed
Salt to taste
¼ cup brandy

Sauté the bacon in a large, heavy saucepan over medium heat for 2 minutes. Add the onions, carrots, shallots, and leek and cook until well browned, about 12 to 15 minutes. Stir in the vinegar and simmer over low heat until the liquid has evaporated, about 10 to 15 minutes. Whisk in the flour and cook one minute more. Then add the garlic, marinade, bouquet garni, and stock. Simmer over low heat for one hour. Stir in the cracked peppercorns and salt and simmer for 10 minutes more. Strain through a chinois. Return to the saucepan and add the brandy. Simmer 3 minutes over low heat and serve hot.

YIELD: ABOUT 2½ CUPS

❧ RAISIN SAUCE

Sweet sauces with pork or game are classic. This one combines a little sweetness with the acidity of vinegar for a delightfully different taste. Serve it with that Easter ham for rave reviews. Prepare this sauce no more than two days in advance and refrigerate it. Rewarm over low heat before serving.

> 3 tablespoons dark brown sugar
> 1 tablespoon Dijon mustard
> 3 tablespoons red wine vinegar
> 1 cup Basic Brown Sauce (page 15)
> 1/4 cup raisins, plumped in 1 cup hot brandy for 10 minutes and drained

In a small bowl, dissolve the sugar and mustard in the vinegar. Place the mixture in a medium-size, heavy saucepan, add the brown sauce, and simmer over low heat for 10 minutes. Stir in the raisins and simmer 5 minutes longer. Serve hot.

YIELD: ABOUT 1 CUP

❧ VELOUTÉ

The delicate taste of this luxurious sauce makes it perfect for creaming poultry, eggs, or elegant edibles such as sweetbreads or oysters.

> 2 tablespoons (1/4 stick) butter
> 1/4 cup flour
> 3 cups White or Veal Stock (page 13), heated to boiling
> 4 whole black peppercorns
> 1/2 cup chopped mushrooms (leftover trimmings and stems can be used)
> Salt and freshly ground black pepper to taste

Melt the butter in a large, heavy saucepan over medium heat. Whisk in the flour and cook for 3 minutes; then stir in the hot stock. Add the peppercorns and mushrooms and simmer gently over low heat at least 30 minutes. Strain through a chinois and season with salt and pepper.

YIELD: ABOUT 2 CUPS

🦋 ROSEMARY SAUCE

Rosemary and lamb seem to go together naturally, whether the herb is sprinkled on chops while grilling, or incorporated in a savory sauce. This sauce is also delicious with cold roast lamb, or any of that butterflied roast left over from the Sunday barbecue. Inspired by a sauce once served at New York City's American Harvest Restaurant, this makes a wonderful addition to summer menus.

> *2 tablespoons (¹/₄ stick) butter*
> *1 large shallot, chopped*
> *1 tablespoon chopped fresh rosemary*
> *¹/₄ cup dry white wine*
> *¹/₂ cup Brown stock (page 11)*
> *¹/₂ cup heavy cream*
> *Salt and freshly ground black pepper to taste*

Heat the butter in a medium-size, heavy skillet over medium heat. Add the shallot and sauté until transparent, about 3 to 4 minutes. Add the rosemary and wine and cook over high heat until most of the liquid has evaporated, about 3 to 4 minutes. Stir in the stock and continue to cook over high heat until the liquid is reduced by half. Add the heavy cream, and season, then boil over medium heat for 3 minutes. Strain through a chinois if you prefer a smooth sauce; do not if a more textured sauce is appropriate. The sauce should be very hot. Serve immediately.

YIELD: ABOUT 1 CUP

✤ STOCK-BASED CURRY SAUCE

Use this pungent sauce for chicken or lamb. The stronger the curry powder used, the more bite the final dish will have. Add a dried red pepper or two if you like fiery hot flavors.

> 3 tablespoons butter
> 1 clove garlic, crushed
> 2 medium-size onions, chopped
> 3 to 4 teaspoons curry powder
> 3 cups Brown Stock (page 11)
> 2 teaspoons Worcestershire sauce
> 1 tablespoon white wine vinegar
> 2 tablespoons flour
> 1/4 cup muscat raisins, plumped in 1/2 cup boiling water for 10 minutes and
>   drained
> Salt and freshly ground black pepper to taste

Melt the butter in a large, heavy saucepan over medium heat. Add the garlic and onions and sauté until transparent, about 5 to 6 minutes. Stir in the curry powder, stock, Worcestershire, and vinegar, and simmer over low heat for 15 to 20 minutes. Blend the flour with a little cold water until smooth, then stir into the sauce and simmer until thickened, about 3 minutes. Add the raisins and season with salt and pepper to taste. Simmer one minute longer and serve immediately.

YIELD: ABOUT 2 CUPS

CHAPTER THREE

❧ *White Sauces*

THE TWO MAJOR TYPES OF WHITE SAUCES ARE BÉCHAMELS AND VELOUTÉS. THE major difference is that a béchamel is made with milk or cream, but a velouté requires a white, chicken, or fish stock. For that reason, you'll find the recipe for basic velouté in Chapter 1, Stocks and Stock-Based Sauces. Normally, velouté sauces have a more pronounced flavor than béchamels.

White sauces made with stock rather than milk or cream can be simmered a longer time to concentrate their flavors if desired. However, 15 to 30 minutes is long enough, as these sauces tend to thicken even more with continued cooking. Keep in mind that white sauces made with milk and cream can burn easily if cooked too long.

In general, white sauces are made with what is called a *roux,* created by first cooking the flour in butter or another fat before adding the liquid. Care must be taken when cooking the flour that the mixture does not brown; it should foam up and be very light in color. The liquid should be added all at once while whisking constantly and should continue to be whisked until it begins to boil. Then the heat should be reduced and the sauce simmered for at least 5 minutes to remove any flavor of uncooked flour. If the liquid is hot before it is added to the roux, it will come to a boil faster and whisking time will be reduced.

This same roux is the secret of Cajun cookery, but in that case the flour and fat mixture is cooked until it is nearly black, a long, slow process that must be watched constantly to prevent the flour from burning. Many Cajun chefs insist that the roux is so important that they prepare it themselves, even if there are others available to finish the dish.

Many chefs no longer make flour-based sauces, insisting on "lighter" preparations. When you consider that many of these sauces contain only a tablespoon or two of flour to two or three cups of liquid, it really is not the flour that is the problem. A lighter sauce can be made by adding more liquid to produce a thinner consistency. Many of the white sauces in this section are just too good to be discarded out of hand—especially those with distinctive flavors, such as onion, curry, mustard, or horseradish, for example. I suggest you experiment with some of these, making them according to the recipe the first time and then adding your own special touches for future uses.

By the way, it is essential to master making a smooth flour-based sauce if you ever plan to prepare a soufflé, as the same type of mixture is the basis for many different soufflés, both savory and sweet.

WHITE SAUCE TIPS

- If whisking the liquid into the roux produces lumps, strain the sauce through a fine sieve before proceeding with the recipe.

- It is easy to alter the consistency of a white sauce. If it's too thin, simply simmer until thick, stirring occasionally. If it's too thick, whisk in more liquid, a little at a time.

- If you are making the white sauce ahead of time (common when making soufflés), rub the surface of the hot sauce with the end of a stick of butter before letting it cool. The resulting thin layer of melted butter will help prevent a skin from forming. If a skin does form, remove it; don't try to beat it into the sauce.

- Any white sauce that does not contain cream or eggs can be stored in the refrigerator for one day or frozen successfully for up to two weeks. Egg yolks have a tendency to separate in a sauce when thawed, and cream-based sauces become thin after having been frozen. If a frozen white sauce has become thin, dissolve 1 to 2 teaspoons arrowroot in 2 tablespoons water and beat it into the hot sauce. It will thicken slightly and should be used right away. Do not cook it for more than a minute or two longer or the sauce will thin out again.

- White sauces can be enriched just before serving by beating in egg yolks. Remember to beat a little of the hot sauce into the eggs before beating them into the sauce itself, or you'll

run the risk of curdling the sauce. Once the eggs have been
added the sauce should not be boiled again, but be served
immediately.

❦ AURORE SAUCE

Aurore is the rosy glow that just precedes the dawn. It is the tomato
concentrate in this cream sauce that gives it the same warm hue. Serve
it with roasted or poached poultry, fish, or eggs.

2 tablespoons (¼ stick) butter
1 tablespoon flour
2 cups milk
2 tablespoons tomato concentrate
Salt and freshly ground white pepper to taste

Melt the butter in a heavy saucepan over medium heat. Add the flour and,
stirring occasionally, cook until frothy, but not browned, about 2 minutes. Add the milk a little at a time, stirring constantly. Simmer gently for
10 minutes.

Just before serving, whisk in the tomato concentrate and season
with salt and pepper.

YIELD: ABOUT 2 CUPS

❦ CREAMY MUSTARD SAUCE

Mustard adds a delicate tang to this classic sauce. Serve it with fish, eggs,
and winter vegetables, such as broccoli and cauliflower.

1 cup Béchamel (page 30), hot
2 tablespoons Dijon mustard
1 tablespoon chopped fresh parsley

Stir the mustard into the white sauce in a small saucepan, add the parsley,
and heat thoroughly, but do not allow to boil.

YIELD: ABOUT 1 CUP.

❧ BÉCHAMEL (BASIC WHITE SAUCE)

This is one of the most basic of sauces. Sometimes used by itself, it is also often employed as a base for more flavorful mixtures. The recipe below can be used as the base for soufflés, for thickening purees, or for creaming vegetables, chicken, tuna, and so on.

> 3 tablespoons butter
> 2 tablespoons minced onion
> 3 tablespoons flour
> 1 1/2 cups milk, scalded (heated just until bubbles form around edge of pan)
> Salt and freshly ground white pepper to taste
> Pinch of ground nutmeg
> 1 teaspoon chopped fresh parsley

Melt the butter in a small saucepan over medium heat. Add the onion and sauté until just transparent, about 4 to 5 minutes. Stir in the flour, and, stirring occasionally, cook until bubbly, but not browned, about 3 minutes.

Whisk in the milk all at once. Season with salt and pepper. Reduce the heat to low and simmer until thick, about 10 minutes. Strain through a sieve, then stir in the nutmeg and parsley.

YIELD: ABOUT 1 1/2 CUPS

❧ BERCY (SHALLOT-FLAVORED CREAM SAUCE)

Here is a delicious combination that adds life to any baked or poached fish.

2 tablespoons (¼ stick) butter
1 tablespoon finely minced shallots
¼ cup dry white wine
1 cup hot Velouté (page 24) made with Fish Stock (page 13)
1 teaspoon butter
1 tablespoon fresh lemon juice
1 tablespoon chopped fresh parsley

Melt the 2 tablespoons butter in a heavy saucepan over medium heat. Add the shallots and cook until transparent, about 5 minutes. Add the wine and simmer over low heat for 3 minutes. Stir in the warm velouté sauce.

Add the remaining butter and the lemon juice and continue cooking until heated through. Stir in the parsley and serve immediately.

YIELD: ABOUT 1 CUP

❦ BREAD SAUCE

If Dickensian novels are your passion, you have no doubt encountered references to this sauce. Here is an updated version, well flavored with onion and thickened with bread. The yeasty onion flavor goes very well with roast turkey or chicken, and surprisingly well with pork.

    4 cups milk
    3 large onions, peeled and quartered
    1 teaspoon whole cloves
    6 slices white bread, crusts removed, torn into small pieces
    Salt and freshly ground white pepper to taste

In a large saucepan over low heat, simmer the onions and cloves in milk for one hour, stirring from time to time. Strain through a strainer, reserving the onions and the milk. Puree the onions with ⅔ of the milk in a food processor or blender. Pour the mixture back into the saucepan, stir in the bread, and then beat in the remaining milk. Simmer over low heat for 20 minutes, stirring from time to time. Season well with salt and pepper, then beat until smooth. Serve hot.

YIELD: ABOUT 2½ CUPS

🦋 CREAMY CURRY SAUCE

This multipurpose sauce goes well with fish, shellfish, eggs, or vegetables, as well as lamb or poultry. Add it to any leftover meat or fish for a quick, stylish dish.

> *2 tablespoons (¹/₄ stick) butter*
> *1 medium-size onion, minced*
> *1 tablespoon flour*
> *2 tablespoons hot curry powder*
> *2 cups Brown Stock (page 11) or White or Veal Stock (page 13)*
> *2 tablespoons heavy cream*
> *Salt and freshly ground white pepper to taste*

Melt the butter in a medium-size, heavy saucepan over medium heat. Add the onion and sauté until just golden, at least 10 minutes. Sprinkle with the flour and curry powder and stir well.

Add the stock a little at a time, mixing thoroughly. Simmer over low heat for about 15 minutes, stirring from time to time.

Stir in the cream and season well with salt and pepper. Continue cooking until heated through.

YIELD: ABOUT 2 CUPS

🦋 DOUBLE MUSTARD SAUCE

This mustard sauce has considerable character. Not only is it made with full-flavored chicken stock, but it contains a double dose of mustard. Put it up against baked ham, roast pork, or grilled fish, or serve it with steamed vegetables.

> *2 tablespoons (¹/₄ stick) butter*
> *1 small onion, minced*
> *1 tablespoon flour*
> *¹/₂ cup Chicken Stock (page 12), boiling*
> *¹/₂ cup milk, scalded (heated just until bubbles form around edges of pan)*
> *3 tablespoons Dijon mustard*
> *1 tablespoon dry mustard*
> *1 teaspoon dark brown sugar*
> *1 teaspoon Worcestershire sauce*

Melt the butter in a medium-size heavy saucepan over medium heat. Add the onion and sauté until soft, about 5 to 8 minutes. Stir in the flour, then the boiling stock and scalded milk. Raise the heat to high, bring to a boil, then lower the heat to medium and cook, stirring, until thick, about 5 minutes. Beat in the mustards, sugar, and Worcestershire sauce and continue cooking just until heated through.

YIELD: ABOUT 1 CUP

EGG SAUCE

Another classic sauce, this one is delicious with poached fish. Stir in a little chopped fresh parsley for additional color.

2 tablespoons (¼ stick) butter
2 tablespoons flour
1 ½ cups milk, scalded (heated just until bubbles form around edges of pan)
1 cup heavy cream
Salt and freshly ground white pepper to taste
2 hard-boiled eggs, peeled and diced

Melt the butter in a medium-size heavy saucepan over medium heat. Add the flour and cook 3 minutes. Add the milk and cook, stirring, until very thick, about 5 or 6 minutes. Stir in the cream and simmer again for 2 minutes.

Just before serving, season well with salt and pepper and stir in the chopped egg.

YIELD: ABOUT 1 CUP

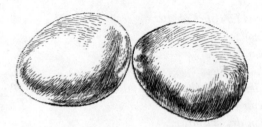

❧ CREAMY GARLIC SAUCE

Garlic lovers will go for this delicious cream sauce. See for yourself what it does for broccoli and other vegetables.

2 tablespoons (¼ stick) butter
3 cloves garlic, minced
2 tablespoons flour
½ cup Chicken Stock (page 12), boiled over high heat until reduced to ¼
   cup
¼ cup dry white wine
1 large egg yolk, beaten
2 tablespoons fresh lemon juice
½ cup heavy cream, whipped to stiff peaks
Salt and freshly ground white pepper to taste

Melt the butter in a medium-size heavy saucepan over medium heat. Add the garlic and cook until soft, about 2 minutes. Stir in the flour, then the reduced stock and wine. Cook until very thick, about 5 to 6 minutes, stirring occasionally.

Whisk about ½ cup of the hot sauce into the beaten egg yolk, then stir the mixture back into the sauce. Add the lemon juice, then fold in the whipped cream and season well with salt and pepper. Serve hot.

YIELD: ABOUT 1 CUP

❦ HOT HORSERADISH SAUCE

Frequently a cold horseradish and cream mixture is served with boiled beef or standing rib roast. This hot horseradish sauce makes a nice change of pace. Try it with hard-boiled eggs, brussels sprouts, or other winter vegetables.

> 2 tablespoons (1/4 stick) butter
> 1 medium-size onion, minced
> 2 tablespoons flour
> 3 cups Brown Stock (page 11), boiled over high heat until reduced to 1 1/2 cups
> 1/4 cup grated fresh horseradish
> 1/4 cup fresh lemon juice
> Pinch of sugar
> Salt and freshly ground white pepper to taste
> 1/2 cup sour cream

Melt the butter in a large, heavy saucepan over medium heat. Add the onion and sauté until transparent, about 5 to 8 minutes. Add the flour and cook for three minutes. Beat in the stock, making a smooth sauce.

Stir in the horseradish, lemon juice, sugar, salt, and pepper. Simmer over low heat until thick, about 10 minutes. Just before serving, stir in the sour cream and heat through, but do not boil.

YIELD: ABOUT 2 CUPS

❦ LEMON MUSTARD SAUCE

Serve this tangy cream sauce over eggs, poached or baked fish, or even
freshly steamed vegetables.

> *4 tablespoons (½ stick) butter*
> *2 tablespoons flour*
> *1½ cups milk*
> *2 large egg yolks*
> *3 tablespoons fresh lemon juice*
> *2 tablespoons Dijon mustard*
> *Red (cayenne) pepper or hot pepper sauce to taste*

Melt the butter in a medium-size saucepan over medium heat. Stir in the
flour and cook for three minutes, but do not allow the mixture to brown.
Add the milk all at once, stirring constantly, and boil until slightly thick,
about 5 minutes. Cover and set aside.

In a medium-size bowl, beat together the egg yolks, lemon juice,
mustard, and pepper. Stir ¼ cup of the hot milk mixture into the egg
yolks. Then pour the egg yolk mixture back into the saucepan. Cook over
medium heat, stirring constantly, until thick, about 3 to 5 minutes. Do not
boil.

YIELD: ABOUT 2 CUPS

❧ MORNAY SAUCE

This truly versatile sauce can be served with almost anything: fish, pasta, eggs, vegetables, poultry. A quick trip under the broiler once a dish has been sauced will result in a golden brown gem—enough to tempt even the most jaded appetite. Named for the Duc de Mornay, this was one of the early flour-thickened sauces in the French repertoire.

> 3 tablespoons butter
> 1 tablespoon flour
> 2 cups milk, scalded (heated just until bubbles form around edges of pan)
> 3 tablespoons freshly grated Parmesan cheese
> 3 tablespoons freshly grated Gruyère cheese
> 1 large egg yolk
> ¼ teaspoon ground nutmeg
> Salt and freshly ground black or white pepper to taste

Melt the butter in a medium-size, heavy saucepan over medium heat. Add the flour and cook until bubbly, but not browned, about 2 minutes. Stir in the hot milk all at once and simmer over low heat until thick and creamy, about 10 minutes. Stir occasionally.

Remove the sauce from the heat. Beat in the cheeses and egg yolk. Season with the nutmeg, salt, and pepper. Serve immediately.

YIELD: ABOUT 2 CUPS

❧ MUSHROOM AND WALNUT SAUCE

This flavorful cream sauce will complement almost any baked or poached fish, as well as poultry or veal.

    3 tablespoons butter
    1 tablespoon minced onion
    ⅔ cup (2 ounces) sliced mushrooms
    2 tablespoons flour
    2 cups half and half, scalded (heated just until bubbles form around edges of
        pan)
    1 tablespoon Dijon mustard
    1 tablespoon chopped fresh thyme or 1 teaspoon dried
    ¼ cup chopped toasted walnuts
    Salt and freshly ground black pepper to taste

Heat the butter in a medium-size, heavy saucepan over medium heat. Add the onion and mushrooms and sauté until the onion is transparent, about 5 to 8 minutes. Stir in the flour, then add the half and half, stirring until smooth. Add the mustard and cook until thickened, about 10 minutes, stirring occasionally. Add the thyme and walnuts and season well with salt and pepper.

    YIELD: ABOUT 2 CUPS

❧ ONION BÉCHAMEL

This delicate variation of the classic sauce is perfect for vegetables.

    1 cup half and half
    ½ cup milk
    2 tablespoons (¼ stick) butter
    2 tablespoons flour
    3 tablespoons minced onion
    2 tablespoons chopped fresh parsley
    Salt and freshly ground white pepper to taste
    1 large egg, beaten

Scald the half and half and milk together in a small, heavy saucepan and set aside. Melt the butter in a medium-size, heavy saucepan over medium heat. Stir in the flour, then add the half and half and milk, stirring constantly. Simmer over low heat until thickened, about 3 minutes, then stir in the onion, parsley, salt, and pepper. Raise the heat to medium and boil the sauce until it is thick, about 6 to 10 minutes.

Remove the sauce from the heat. Beat about ½ cup of the hot sauce into the beaten egg yolk; then pour the egg yolk mixture back into the sauce, stirring constantly. Simmer the sauce gently over low heat until it has thickened once more, about 3 minutes; do not allow it to boil. Serve immediately.

YIELD: ABOUT 1½ CUPS

❦ NEWBURG SAUCE

Created by a chef at the now defunct Delmonico's Restaurant in New York City, this sauce was meant to accompany lobster. At that time, lobster was not the festive dish it is today, and unctuous sauces were used to elevate that "common" shellfish to the realm of something special. This sauce is equally good with shrimp, lotte (monkfish), and other seafood.

3 tablespoons butter
2 large shallots, minced
½ cup dry sherry
1 cup Velouté (page 24) made with Fish Stock (page 13)
½ cup heavy cream
2 large egg yolks, beaten
Salt and freshly ground white pepper to taste

Melt the butter in a medium-size, heavy saucepan over medium heat. Add the shallots and sauté until transparent, about 3 to 5 minutes. Stir in sherry then stir in the velouté sauce. In a small bowl, beat the cream into the egg yolks, then stir into the hot sauce. Heat the sauce through, stirring constantly, over low heat; do not allow it to come to a boil. Season with salt and pepper.

YIELD: ABOUT 2 CUPS

❧ PARSLEY SAUCE

This garlicky sauce adds a special, tangy taste to any kind of shellfish.

> 2 tablespoons olive oil
> 1/4 cup minced onion
> 3 cloves garlic, minced
> 2 teaspoons flour
> 3/4 cup dry white wine
> 3/4 cup chopped fresh parsley
> Salt and freshly ground white pepper to taste

Heat the oil in a heavy saucepan over medium heat. Add the onion and garlic and sauté until transparent, about 5 to 8 minutes. Stir in the flour, then add the wine and cook until the sauce is thick, about 5 minutes. Stir in the parsley and season well with salt and pepper.

YIELD: ABOUT 1 CUP

❧ POULETTE SAUCE

A classic French sauce, this creamy mixture goes equally as well with fish and shellfish as it does with veal or sweetbreads.

> 3 tablespoons butter
> 4 1/2 teaspoons flour
> 2 cups White or Veal Stock (page 13), heated to boiling
> 1/4 cup chopped mushrooms (leftover stems and trimmings can be used instead of whole mushrooms)
> 2 tablespoons fresh lemon juice
> 2 large egg yolks, beaten
> 2 tablespoons chopped fresh parsley
> Salt and freshly ground white pepper to taste

In a medium-size, heavy saucepan, melt the butter over medium heat and add the flour. Cook until bubbly, but not brown, about 2 minutes. Add the hot stock all at once, stirring constantly. Stir in the mushrooms and simmer gently over low heat for 20 minutes. Remove from heat and strain through a sieve, pressing on the mushrooms to extract as much liquid as possible. Discard mushrooms. In a small bowl, beat the lemon juice into the yolks. Then beat in ¼ cup of the hot sauce and pour the egg mixture back into the remaining sauce, stirring constantly. Do not reheat. Stir in the parsley and season well with salt and pepper. Serve at once.

YIELD: ABOUT 1½ CUPS

✿ RAVIGOTE SAUCE (HOT)

This is an important sauce in the French kitchen. It can accompany boiled beef, roast pork, roast chicken, sweetbreads, or even hard-boiled eggs.

⅓ cup white wine vinegar
2 large shallots, minced
2 tablespoons chopped fresh chives
1½ cups White or Veal Stock (page 13) or Chicken Stock (page 12)
2 tablespoons (¼ stick) butter, melted
1 tablespoon flour
Salt and freshly ground black or white pepper to taste
1 large egg yolk, beaten
1 tablespoon chopped fresh chervil
1 tablespoon chopped fresh parsley
1 tablespoon chopped fresh tarragon

In a small, heavy saucepan, over high heat, bring the vinegar, shallots, and chives to a boil and reduce until only one tablespoon of liquid is left. Strain the reduction through a small strainer and stir it into the stock. Set aside.

Melt the butter in a small, heavy saucepan over medium heat. Add the flour and cook, stirring, for 3 minutes. Then, little by little, add the stock, stirring constantly. Season well and simmer over low heat for 5 minutes.

Beat about ¼ cup of the hot sauce into the beaten egg yolk; then pour the egg yolk mixture back into the remaining sauce, stirring constantly. Add the herbs and heat the sauce through over low heat, but do not let it boil. Serve very hot.

YIELD: ABOUT 1 CUP

❧ ROQUEFORT SAUCE

You will want to use this easy, but very savory sauce over lamb, veal, baked or roast potatoes, and even broccoli or cauliflower.

2 tablespoons (¼ stick) butter
2 tablespoons flour
¼ cup crumbled Roquefort cheese
1 cup White or Veal Stock (page 13)
Salt and freshly ground white pepper to taste

In a small bowl, mash together the butter and flour with a fork. Add the Roquefort cheese and mix until creamy. Set aside.

Bring the stock to a boil in a small, heavy saucepan. Reduce the heat to low and add the Roquefort mixture a little at a time, beating constantly. Continue to beat the sauce until smooth. Simmer gently for 15 minutes to incorporate the flavors and thicken. If the sauce becomes too thick, beat in a little more stock.

Season well with salt and pepper, but remember that the Roquefort cheese is already quite salty.

YIELD: ABOUT 1 CUP

❦ SAUCE NANTUA

Not a busy day sauce, this one requires some preparation, unless your freezer is stocked with all the basics. For special occasions serve this with poached fish or shellfish, hard-boiled or poached eggs—or even shirred eggs, for a change.

> *3 tablespoons Shrimp Butter (page 97)*
> *1 medium-size or large, ripe tomato, peeled, seeded, and finely chopped*
> *¼ cup heavy cream*
> *2 tablespoons cognac*
> *2 cups Béchamel (page 30), hot*
> *Hot pepper sauce to taste*
> *Salt and freshly ground white pepper to taste*

Melt the shrimp butter in a medium-size, heavy saucepan over low heat. Add the tomato and sauté several minutes, until soft. In a medium-size mixing bowl, combine the cream, cognac, and béchamel; then stir in the tomato mixture. Season well with the hot pepper sauce, salt, and pepper.

YIELD: ABOUT 2 CUPS

❦ SMITANE SAUCE

Traditionally, this sauce is served with pheasant or other game birds. If you are lucky enough to have a hunter at home, it will become a mainstay of your game menus. It is also delicious with domestic duck or lamb.

> 2 tablespoons (1/4 stick) butter
> 1 large shallot, minced
> 1/2 small onion, minced
> 2 tablespoons white wine vinegar
> 1 cup heavy cream
> 1/4 cup Béchamel (page 30), hot
> Salt and freshly ground white pepper to taste

In a medium-size, heavy saucepan, sauté the shallots and onion in the butter over medium heat until transparent, about 5 to 8 minutes. Stir in the vinegar, bring the mixture to a boil, and reduce it until most of the liquid has evaporated.

Stir in the cream and continue to cook over medium heat until the sauce has been reduced by half. Remove from the heat and stir in the béchamel sauce. Season with salt and pepper; serve immediately.

YIELD: ABOUT 3/4 CUP

❦ SOUBISE SAUCE

The rich onion flavor of this classic French sauce makes it a perfect partner for fish, poultry, chicken, even roast pork.

> 2 tablespoons (1/4 stick) butter
> 2 large onions, thinly sliced or chopped
> 1 1/2 cups Béchamel (page 30)
> 1/2 cup heavy cream
> Salt and freshly ground black or white pepper to taste
> Pinch of ground nutmeg

Melt the butter in a large, heavy saucepan over medium heat. Add onions and cook until extremely soft, but not browned, about 20 minutes. Stir in the béchamel sauce and simmer gently over low heat for 15 minutes.

Remove the sauce from the heat and strain if a smooth sauce is desired (do not strain if you wish a more robust consistency). Return to low heat and stir in the cream; heat through. Season well with salt, pepper, and nutmeg.

YIELD: ABOUT 2 CUPS

❦ SUPREME SAUCE

Maybe this really is a supreme sauce—it certainly is rich and creamy. If calories are of no concern, serve it with game, poultry, lamb, green vegetables, or almost anything.

> 3 tablespoons butter
> 2 tablespoons flour
> 1 cup Chicken Stock (page 12), heated to boiling
> 1/4 pound mushrooms, washed, dried, and minced
> Salt and freshly ground white pepper to taste
> 2 large egg yolks, beaten
> 1/3 cup heavy cream
> 2 teaspoons fresh lemon juice

Melt the butter in a small, heavy saucepan over medium heat. Add the flour and stir until bubbly, but not browned, about 2 to 3 minutes. Add the stock all at once, stirring constantly. Then add the mushrooms and season with salt and pepper.

Simmer the sauce over low heat for 20 minutes or until reduced by about one third. While it is simmering, beat the egg yolks, cream, and lemon juice together in a small bowl.

Remove the sauce from the heat and beat the egg mixture into it. Then return it to the stove and cook gently over low heat for several minutes to heat the sauce through; do not let it boil.

YIELD: ABOUT 1 CUP

CHAPTER FOUR

❧ *Wine Sauces*

WHILE WINE CAN BE ADDED TO MANY SAUCES, THIS SECTION IS A COLLECTION of those that owe their very distinctive flavor to the the wine that is used in them. As a result, it's important to use a wine that you would be satisfied to drink. That doesn't mean you have to break out a bottle of fine Bordeaux, but the shorter the cooking time and the less the sauce is reduced, the better the wine should be.

Most people should have no problem with cooked sauces that incorporate wine, since the alcohol is evaporated by heating the mixture. All that will be left is the essence of the wine's flavor. Just cook the sauce for several minutes to be sure that the alcohol has evaporated, otherwise it will leave an unpleasant raw taste.

❧ APPLE CREAM SAUCE

Fruit and game tend to go together well. Serve this special sauce with game, including boar, bear, and wild birds—or partner it with domestic duck or roast pork.

> 1 cup fresh apple cider
> 2 medium-size Golden Delicious apples, peeled, cored, and sliced
> 1/2 cup sweet white wine
> 1 cup White or Veal Stock (page 13) or Chicken Stock (page 12)
> 1/4 cup applejack or other apple brandy
> 2 tablespoons (1/4 stick) butter
> 2 tablespoons chopped fresh tarragon
> 1/2 cup heavy cream
> Salt and freshly ground black or white pepper to taste

In a large, heavy saucepan, boil the cider over high heat until it has been reduced to ½ cup. Reduce heat to medium, add the apples, wine, and stock, and continue to boil until the apples fall apart (the sauce will be a bit chunky). Then adjust the heat to low and stir in the applejack, butter, and tarragon. Simmer the sauce for 5 minutes. Stir in the cream and simmer 5 minutes more. Season well with salt and pepper. The sauce should be very hot. Serve immediately.

YIELD: ABOUT 2 CUPS

❦ BASIC RED WINE SAUCE

Learn to make this sauce and you will have at your fingertips the means to make any ordinary dish a special one. The wine is cooked long enough to eliminate any raw taste and the remaining yeasty fruit flavor is excellent with many beef, egg, and even fish dishes. This sauce can be prepared up to two days in advance and refrigerated. Rewarm over low heat before serving.

> 2 cups dry red wine
> 3 large shallots, minced
> 1 bouquet garni
> 1 tablespoon flour
> 6 tablespoons (¾ stick) butter
> Pinch of red (cayenne) pepper or hot pepper sauce to taste
> Salt to taste

In a medium-size, heavy saucepan over high heat, boil the red wine, shallots, and bouquet garni for 10 minutes. Strain the sauce and bring it to a boil again. In the meantime, in a small bowl, cream the flour and 2 tablespoons of the butter together to make a smooth paste. Add this paste to the boiling wine a little at a time, stirring after each addition until smooth. Then adjust the heat to low and simmer the sauce until thick, about 3 minutes.

Remove the sauce from the heat and whisk in the remaining butter a little at a time. The butter will cool the sauce slightly and emulsify easily. Do not overheat or let the butter melt. The sauce should be light and creamy. Season with the red pepper and salt. Serve warm.

YIELD: ABOUT 1½ CUPS

❧ LEMON WINE SAUCE

This sweet and savory sauce enhances the flavor of all kinds of poultry and grilled fish. If desired, it can be made one or two days in advance and stored in the refrigerator. Rewarm it over low heat before serving.

   1 tablespoon olive oil
   1 teaspoon grated fresh ginger
   1 tablespoon chopped lemon (both rind and pulp)
   ½ cup Chicken Stock (page 12)
   ½ cup dry white wine
   1 tablespoon honey
   ¼ cup fresh lemon juice
   1 teaspoon soy sauce

Heat the oil in a small, heavy saucepan over medium heat. Stir in the ginger and chopped lemon and sauté for one minute. Then stir in the stock, wine, honey, and lemon juice. Simmer over low heat for 15 minutes and add the soy sauce. Serve hot.

   YIELD: ABOUT 1 CUP

❧ MUSCOVITE SAUCE

Take the time to make this sauce and serve it with venison, wild goose, or other game.

   2 cups Pepper Sauce (Poivrade) (page 23), boiled over medium heat for 10
      minutes to reduce it slightly
   ½ cup Madeira
   2 tablespoons chopped almonds, toasted
   2 tablespoons raisins, plumped in ¼ cup boiling water for 10 minutes, and
      drained

Combine all the ingredients in a small, heavy saucepan and simmer over low heat for 3 minutes. The sauce should be very hot. Serve immediately.

   YIELD: ABOUT 2 CUPS

❧ TARRAGON CREAM SAUCE

The anise flavor of tarragon can perk up the delicate flavor of roast or poached chicken. Or try this sauce with grilled, baked, or poached fish. Spoon a little onto the plate and place the meat or fish on top. Then just a dollop more on top will accentuate the dish without masking its own flavor.

> 3 tablespoons butter
> 2 large shallots, minced
> 2 cloves garlic, minced
> 3/4 cup dry white wine
> 2 tablespoons fresh lemon juice
> 1/2 cup Chicken Stock (page 12)
> 1/4 cup heavy cream
> 3 tablespoons minced fresh tarragon

Heat the butter in a medium-size, heavy saucepan over medium heat. Add the shallots and garlic and sauté until they are just transparent, but not browned, about 5 to 8 minutes. Add the wine, lemon juice, and stock and bring to a boil over high heat. Continue to boil until the liquid is reduced to about 1/2 cup.

Adjust the heat to low and stir in the cream and tarragon. Heat through and serve immediately.

YIELD: ABOUT 1 CUP

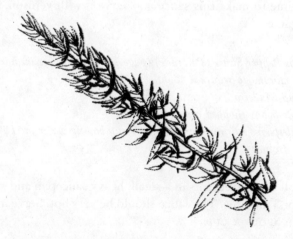

❦ SAFFRON SAUCE

Saffron may be the most expensive seasoning in the world. Any sauce that incorporates it automatically takes on a richness and festivity all its own. Serve this luscious sauce with fish or shellfish to satisfy even the most discerning tastes.

½ cup dry white wine
¼ cup dry vermouth
½ cup Chicken Stock (page 12)
3 large shallots, minced
⅛ teaspoon saffron
½ cup heavy cream
Salt and freshly ground black pepper

In a heavy saucepan, bring the wine, vermouth, stock, shallots, and saffron to a boil over high heat and continue to cook until the liquid is reduced to ½ cup. Stir in the cream and cook over medium heat until just slightly thickened, at least 10 minutes. Season with salt and pepper and serve immediately.

YIELD: ABOUT 1 CUP

CHAPTER FIVE

❧ *Emulsified Butter Sauces*

IF ANY SAUCES STRIKE FEAR INTO THE HEARTS OF FIRST-TIME SAUCEMAKERS, they are hollandaise, béarnaise, beurre blanc, and all their relatives. They have a reputation for being difficult to make, easy to spoil, and prone to separation. While all of these things are true if the saucemaker is uninformed or careless, it's really quite easy to make stunningly smooth examples of these sauces with very little effort.

The primary lesson to learn is that high heat is anathema. If you remember that all of the "hot" emulsified sauces are in reality served warm, not hot, it's simple to create them. Too much heat will melt the butter and destroy the emulsification. When this happens, the sauce separates and the butter appears as a liquid instead of the thick, frothy light-colored mixture that you are looking for. It doesn't matter if the butter is icy cold, or nearly room temperature, but when you are beginning it may be advantageous to use cold butter. That way, each addition will cool the sauce slightly, and lessen the chance the butter will melt.

It is important that the pan you use never becomes too hot. While some cooks use a double boiler, I find that this offers a false sense of security. For me, it is much easier simply to keep moving the pan on and off the heat while beating in the butter. Some old-time French chefs say that the pan should never become too hot to touch.

These are delicate sauces, in both taste and texture. While they contain an enormous amount of butter, and therefore are not "light" at all, it is the combination of acid (from the wine or vinegar and shallots or onions) and fat that produces the silky texture.

Hollandaise, béarnaise, and their derivatives contain eggs and will curdle as well as separate. But once again, it is heat that is the culprit.

Heat is also a problem when serving the finished sauce. Except for some egg dishes, such as Eggs Benedict, these sauces should be served in a separate dish so that the food is not too hot for them when they are put together. Spooning these sauces over boiling hot food also will cause them to separate.

One method for making egg-based emulsions that almost eliminates the problem of curdling is to thoroughly cook the eggs before adding the butter. In this method the butter is melted, strained to eliminate the milk solids, and then added to the eggs in a steady stream. The eggs have been beaten with two or three tablespoons of water or cooking liquid from the food the sauce will accompany and whisked over low heat until the mixture is very light and frothy and almost the color of lemons. It should fall from the whisk in a ribbon, or sheet, when it is ready. This takes about 4 or 5 minutes.

Remove the pan from the heat and beat in a little of the melted and slightly cooled butter until the mixture begins to thicken like mayonnaise. Then beat in the remaining butter in a steady stream. Once all the butter is incorporated, the seasonings can be added. The sauce will now be the correct temperature to serve. While this is a slightly unorthodox method, many professional chefs prefer it because it is nearly foolproof and saves a lot of time.

Sometimes, however, an egg-based emulsification will separate, no matter how careful you've been. Here are three ways to save it:

1. Remove the pan from the heat and beat in an ice cube or a tablespoon or two of icy cold water.

2. Place a tablespoon of cold water in a clean pan and beat in the separated sauce a little at a time until the emulsification begins again, then beat in the rest of the sauce in a steady stream.

3. Start again with one egg yolk beaten with one tablespoon of water and whisked over very low heat until it is light, frothy, and falls from the whisk in a sheet or ribbon. Then, beat in the separated sauce, a little at a time.

If all of this is still too daunting, try the Blender Hollandaise method on page 56 and use it as a base for all the other flavored egg-based sauces in this chapter. There is a slight difference in texture and flavor, but it's quite easy to make.

Beurre blanc and the related "mounted butter" sauces (those that gain volume from the emulsification process and the air that is beaten in) can be stabilized from the beginning by adding a tablespoon of heavy cream to the reduced acid mixture (the lemon juice or vinegar mixture which has been boiled with herbs) before beginning to incorporate the butter.

If a "mounted butter" sauce separates, there is no way to save it. Simply use the flavored butter in some other way.

EMULSIFIED BUTTER SAUCE TIPS

- Keep the sauces warm in a hot water bath. Fill a pan with hot, but not boiling, water and place the pan filled with the sauce in the water. This will maintain the temperature without overheating. Some people like to spoon the finished sauce into a Thermos container which will keep the temperature stable for an hour or two. Do not keep the sauce warm on an open burner and do not try to reheat the sauce once it has cooled.

- Leftover emulsified butter sauces can be used to enrich other sauces. A tablespoon or two beaten into a finished sauce will add a shine and silky texture that is really wonderful.

❧ ANCHOVY BUTTER

For those who love the salty fish flavor of anchovies, this could easily become a favorite. It is sensational on grilled fish.

5 anchovy fillets, rinsed, dried, and mashed into a paste
1/4 pound (1 stick) cold butter, cut into tablespoons
1/2 cup dry sherry
1 teaspoon fresh lemon juice
2 tablespoons chopped capers
1 teaspoon chopped fresh chervil
1 tablespoon chopped fresh parsley
Salt and freshly ground black pepper to taste

In a medium-size, heavy saucepan over medium heat, simmer the anchovies, 1 tablespoon of the butter, the sherry, lemon juice and capers until the liquid has been reduced by one third, about 6 to 8 minutes. Lower the heat. Whisk in the remaining butter several tablespoons at a time, taking care not to let the sauce overheat; the butter should not melt. Remove the saucepan from the heat from time to time if necessary. Beat in the herbs and season well with salt and pepper. Serve warm.

YIELD: ABOUT 1 CUP.

🦋 BEURRE BLANC

This classic French sauce is delicious with many foods. Most often it is served with fish, shellfish, or poultry, but it's perfect with green vegetables as well.

¼ cup white wine vinegar
1 teaspoon minced shallots
4 tablespoons (½ stick) cold butter, cut into 8 pieces
Salt and freshly ground white pepper

In a small, heavy saucepan over high heat boil the vinegar and shallots together until only 2 tablespoons of the liquid remain. Reduce the heat to low and whisk in the butter a little at a time, taking care not to allow the butter to overheat and melt. Remove the saucepan from the heat from time to time if necessary. The sauce should be light and creamy. Season well with salt and pepper.

If you desire a smoother sauce, strain it through a fine sieve. Serve warm, not hot.

YIELD: ABOUT ⅔ CUP

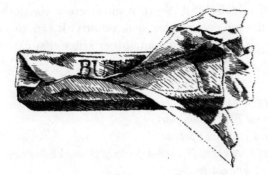

❧ BEURRE ROUGE

This sauce is similar to beurre blanc, but it's heartier and can stand up to beef preparations as well as salmon, monkfish, and even some shellfish.

> *1 cup dry red wine*
> *¼ cup red wine vinegar*
> *1 teaspoon chopped fresh tarragon*
> *1 tablespoon chopped fresh parsley*
> *1 teaspoon whole black peppercorns*
> *½ pound (2 sticks) cold butter, cut into at least 16 pieces*

In a large, heavy saucepan over high heat, boil together the red wine, vinegar, herbs, and peppercorns until the liquid has been reduced to ¼ cup, about 10 minutes. Adjust the heat to low and whisk in the butter a little at a time, removing the pan from the heat periodically so that the butter does not melt. The sauce should be light and creamy and a deep pink color.

Strain the sauce through a fine sieve and keep it warm in a hot water bath (see page 54 for instructions). Serve warm.

YIELD: ABOUT 1½ CUPS

❧ BLENDER HOLLANDAISE

There is no longer any reason to stay away from hollandaise when you have a blender in the kitchen. While this is not as fluffy as classic hollandaise, the flavor is delightful. Serve it anywhere a classic hollandaise is called for—with eggs, vegetables, fish, poultry. It can also be used as a base for Béarnaise, or to enrich any other sauce that calls for butter at the end.

> *3 large egg yolks*
> *2 tablespoons fresh lemon juice*
> *Pinch of red (cayenne) pepper*
> *¼ pound (1 stick) butter, melted, strained through a fine sieve, and kept very warm, but not boiling*

Place the egg yolks, lemon juice, and cayenne in the bowl of a blender and blend thoroughly for about 10 seconds. With the machine on, slowly pour in the warm butter. Blend until thickened. Serve warm or at room temperature.

YIELD: ABOUT 1 CUP

❦ BUTTER HERB SAUCE

The fragrant combination of fresh herbs in this sauce makes it a perfect companion for fish and shellfish.

½ cup dry white wine
2 tablespoons white wine vinegar
2 small shallots, finely minced
2 tablespoons heavy cream
1 teaspoon chopped fresh thyme
¼ pound (1 stick) cold butter, cut into at least 8 pieces
Salt and freshly ground white pepper to taste
1 teaspoon chopped fresh basil
1 teaspoon chopped fresh chives
1 tablespoon chopped fresh parsley

In a medium-size, heavy saucepan over high heat, boil the wine, vinegar, shallots, cream, and thyme together until the liquid has been reduced to ¼ cup, about 3 to 4 minutes. Reduce the heat to low and beat in the butter a little at a time until the sauce is thick and creamy, taking care not to let the butter overheat and melt. Remove the pan from the heat from time to time, if necessary.

Season well with salt and pepper and stir in the remaining herbs. Serve warm, not hot.

YIELD: ABOUT 1 CUP

❦ CHORON SAUCE

Make this with Blender Béarnaise, and it becomes a sophisticated sauce that can be prepared in 5 minutes. Serve it with grilled meat, broiled or poached fish, or broiled poultry.

> *1 cup Easy Béarnaise (page 59), warm*
> *1/4 cup very thick tomato sauce, homemade, if possible (see Index)*

Stir the tomato sauce into the bearnaise and beat well. Serve warm or cold.

YIELD: ABOUT 1 CUP

❦ CLASSIC HOLLANDAISE

A truly multipurpose sauce, this classic hollandaise can be paired with fish, vegetables, or eggs. Use it as the base for other sauces, too. For other methods of making hollandaise, see the introduction to this chapter, and page 56.

> *3 large egg yolks, slightly beaten*
> *1 tablespoon fresh lemon juice*
> *1/2 pound (2 sticks) cold butter, cut into tablespoons*
> *Salt to taste*

In a large, heavy saucepan, beat the egg yolks and lemon juice with a whisk over low heat until very light and creamy. Whisk in the butter a little at a time, being sure the pan never gets hot enough to melt the butter. Remove it from heat from time to time, if necessary.

Continue beating until all butter has been added. The butter should not melt and the sauce should be thick and creamy. Season and serve warm, not hot.

YIELD: ABOUT 2 CUPS

❧ EASY BÉARNAISE

Make this with either Classic Hollandaise (page 58) or Blender Hollandaise (page 56)—whichever you prefer. Classically served with beef, especially chateaubriand or filet mignon, it goes well with any type of steak or fish.

> 2 large shallots, minced
> 2 teaspoons chopped fresh tarragon
> 2 teaspoons chopped fresh chervil or parsley
> 1/4 cup dry white wine
> Salt and freshly ground black pepper to taste
> 1 cup hollandaise, kept warm

Combine the shallots, tarragon, chervil, white wine, salt, and pepper in a small, heavy saucepan and boil over high heat until the liquid has been reduced by half. Remove from the heat and strain through a fine sieve, if desired. Cool slightly and beat the mixture into the warm hollandaise. If desired, beat in a few chopped fresh herbs.

YIELD: ABOUT 1 CUP

❧ HAZELNUT BUTTER SAUCE

Nut lovers will want to put this on everything, but it is truly perfect with grilled fish.

> 2 cloves garlic, minced
> 2 tablespoons fresh lemon juice
> 3 tablespoons dry white wine
> 1/2 cup hazelnuts, toasted and chopped
> 1/4 pound (1 stick) butter, cut into tablespoons
> 3 tablespoons minced fresh parsley
> Freshly ground black or white pepper to taste

In a heavy saucepan over high heat, boil the garlic, lemon juice, and wine until the liquid has been reduced by half. Adjust the heat to low, and stir in the hazelnuts. Then whisk in butter a little at a time. Take care not to let the butter overheat and melt. Remove the pan from the heat from time to time, if necessary. The sauce should be light and creamy. Stir in the parsley and season well with pepper. Serve warm.

YIELD: ABOUT 1 CUP

❧ HOT PEPPER BLENDER HOLLANDAISE

Serve this with shellfish or vegetables.

1/3 cup dry white wine
2 large shallots, minced
2 tablespoons red wine vinegar
1/2 teaspoon crushed red pepper
2 large egg yolks
1 teaspoon fresh lemon juice
1/4 pound (1 stick) butter, melted
Hot pepper sauce to taste

In a small, heavy saucepan over high heat, boil together the wine, shallots, vinegar, and red pepper until the liquid has been reduced to about 2 tablespoons, about 3 to 4 minutes. Then pour the mixture into a blender.

Add the egg yolks and lemon juice, and with the blender on, slowly pour in the melted butter. Blend until smooth and thick. Season to taste with hot pepper sauce. Serve lukewarm.

YIELD: ABOUT 1 CUP

❧ MALTAISE SAUCE

This hollandaise derivative is wonderful over steamed asparagus as a first course. Serve it with other vegetables as well, and with poached fish.

1 cup Classic Hollandaise (page 58), kept warm
3 tablespoons fresh orange juice
1 tablespoon grated orange zest

Beat orange juice and zest into warm hollandaise. Serve at once.

YIELD: ABOUT 1 CUP

MINT HOLLANDAISE

Wonderful with steamed or simmered vegetables, this is also delicious with poached eggs.

1 tablespoon Mint Sauce (page 175)
2 tablespoons chopped fresh mint
1 cup Classic Hollandaise (page 58), kept warm

Stir the mint sauce and fresh mint into the hollandaise. Serve warm.
YIELD: ABOUT 1 CUP

MOUSSELINE SAUCE

Here is a rich, fluffy sauce that is perfect when calories are not a problem. Serve it over eggs or fresh vegetables, but try it with poached salmon for a real treat.

1/4 cup heavy cream, whipped to stiff peaks
1 cup Classic Hollandaise (page 58), kept warm

Fold the whipped cream into the warm Hollandaise. Serve immediately.
YIELD: ABOUT 2 CUPS

❧ PISTACHIO BUTTER SAUCE

The slightly sweet taste of pistachios makes this a perfect partner for grilled fish.

> 6 tablespoons (¾ stick) cold butter, cut into tablespoons
> 1 bunch scallions, chopped
> ½ cup dry white wine
> 1 tablespoon fresh lemon juice
> ½ cup Fish Stock (page 13)
> ¼ cup chopped pistachios
> Salt and freshly ground black pepper to taste

Melt two tablespoons of the butter in a medium-size, heavy saucepan over medium heat. Add the scallions and sauté for 2 minutes. Add the wine, lemon juice, and fish stock and boil over high heat until the liquid is reduced to ½ cup. Reduce heat to low and whisk in the remaining butter one piece at a time until the sauce is smooth and creamy, taking care not to let the butter overheat and melt. Stir in the pistachios and season well with salt and pepper. Serve warm.

YIELD: ABOUT 1½ CUPS

❧ PORT WINE SAUCE

Beef, game, and duck are all great vehicles for this slightly sweet sauce.

> 1½ cups port wine
> ½ cup Brown Stock (page 11)
> 3 large shallots, minced
> ¼ cup heavy cream
> 4 tablespoons (½ stick) cold butter, cut into tablespoons
> Salt and freshly ground black pepper to taste

In a medium-size, heavy saucepan over high heat, boil together the port, stock, and shallots until the liquid is reduced to ½ cup. Stir in the cream and heat the mixture through. Then reduce the heat to low and whisk in the butter, 2 tablespoons at a time, until all the butter has been incorporated and the sauce is thick and creamy. Take care not to let the butter overheat and melt, removing the pan from the heat from time to time if necessary. Season well with salt and pepper. Serve warm.

YIELD: ABOUT 1¼ CUPS

❧ SAUCE MEUNIÈRE

While this is not an emulsified sauce, it does use melted butter and is generally served with poached, sautéed, or grilled fish.

¼ pound (1 stick) butter, melted
2 tablespoons fresh lemon juice
2 tablespoons chopped fresh parsley

Melt the butter in a small, heavy saucepan over medium heat and cook until it turns golden brown, taking care not to let it burn, about 4 to 6 minutes. Beat in the lemon juice and parsley. Serve immediately.

YIELD: ABOUT ½ CUP

CHAPTER SIX

❧ *Mayonnaises*

MAYONNAISE IS SURPRISINGLY SIMPLE TO MAKE. AND ONCE YOU HAVE TASTED the difference between homemade and commercially made mayonnaise, you will want to make your own, especially when using it for salads, or serving with cold poached fish or chicken.

Mayonnaise is much easier to make than hot emulsified sauces like hollandaise. There is no heat to contend with, only the careful addition of oil to an acid mixture of lemon juice or vinegar, mustard, and egg yolks. Just keep in mind the following tips and be sure that all your ingredients are at room temperature.

MAYONNAISE TIPS

● You can use any type of oil (vegetable, olive, or nut) or combination of oils to make most of the recipes in this section. Nut oils, such as walnut, hazelnut, or almond, give the mayonnaise a delicate, slightly nutty taste. If you choose olive oil, use the best quality you can find. Extra-virgin olive oil is now widely available, but if you can't find it, you can also use virgin or cold-pressed.

● The secret to successful mayonnaise is to add the oil drop by drop at the beginning so that the emulsification has a chance to form correctly. Once the mixture begins to thicken and whiten, the oil can be added in a thin, but steady, stream.

If the oil is added too quickly, the sauce will separate. If this happens, you can either place ½ teaspoon prepared mustard OR 1 teaspoon vinegar OR an egg yolk that has been beaten until light in a clean mixing bowl and whisk the separated sauce into it a little at a time until the emulsification begins again, then beat in the remaining mayonnaise a tablespoon at a time.

- Once all the oil has been beaten into the sauce, more flavoring can be added. If a sharper sauce is desired, beat in more lemon juice just before serving.

- Mayonnaise sauces should be served at room temperature so that their full flavor comes through.

- Mayonnaise can be kept, covered, in the warmest part of the refrigerator for 2 to 3 days. Any longer, and it will separate and cannot be reemulsified. Mayonnaise cannot be frozen.

❧ ANCHOVY MAYONNAISE

This sauce really brings out the flavor of grilled fish. Cold roasted or barbecued lamb also seems to profit greatly from a little of this salty sauce with its fresh taste of the sea. Serve it with fresh raw vegetables at your next cocktail party—it will be an unexpected hit. Anchovies are said to stimulate the appetite, so it's wise to make plenty.

1/2 cup soft white bread crumbs
3 tablespoons white wine or cider vinegar
1 large bunch parsley, coarsely chopped
1 clove garlic
3 anchovy fillets
1/3 cup olive oil
Salt and freshly ground black pepper to taste

Soak the bread crumbs in the vinegar for 10 minutes, then squeeze out the excess moisture with your hands. Puree the crumbs, parsley, garlic, and anchovies in a food processor. With the machine running, add all the olive oil a little at a time, and process until the sauce is thick and creamy. Season well with salt and pepper. Serve at room temperature.

YIELD: ABOUT 1 CUP

❧ AIOLI

While it probably originated in Spain, aioli is generally thought of as a sauce from the Provençal region in the south of France. This pungent mixture can be served with boiled fish, potatoes, green beans, hard-boiled eggs—almost anything that benefits from a touch of garlic. Spread it on a toasted slice of French bread and float it on top of a hearty fish soup or bouillabaise. Or use it as a condiment on cold roast pork or beef sandwiches.

> 8 *cloves garlic, crushed (or fewer, according to taste)*
> 2 *large egg yolks*
> 1 *cup olive oil*
> 3 *tablespoons fresh lemon juice*
> 1 *tablespoon warm water*
> *Salt to taste*

In a food processor, process the garlic until smooth by dropping the cloves through the feed tube with the motor running. Add the egg yolks and pulse to mix. With the processor on, add the olive oil a little at a time until the mixture begins to thicken (you may have some olive oil left over). Then stop the machine and add the lemon juice and water. Pulse to mix. With the processor running again, add the remaining olive oil in a steady stream. The mixture should be fairly thick. Season and serve at room temperature.

YIELD: ABOUT 1 CUP

🎋 APPLE MAYONNAISE

This is a terrific sauce to serve with fruit salads, especially those made with citrus. For a delicious surprise, serve it with cold roasted pork or lamb, or spread it on turkey sandwiches.

2 Granny Smith apples, peeled, cored, and sliced
¼ cup fresh mint leaves
½ cup dry white wine
1 cup Basic Mayonnaise (page 68)
1 tablespoon grated fresh horseradish
1 teaspoon Dijon mustard
Salt and freshly ground black pepper to taste

In a large, heavy saucepan, over low heat, simmer the apples and mint in the wine until very tender, about 15 minutes or longer. Transfer the mixture to a blender or food processor and puree. Cool completely, then fold into the mayonnaise and stir in the horseradish and mustard. Season to taste. Serve at room temperature.

YIELD: ABOUT 2 CUPS

🎋 BASIC MACHINE MAYONNAISE

Most food processors require too much liquid to make small quantities of mayonnaise. So, if you want to halve this recipe, you'll have to use a very small model or a blender.

1 tablespoon Dijon mustard
3 large eggs
½ teaspoon salt
2 tablespoons fresh lemon juice
1½ to 2 cups oil, all vegetable, all olive, or a mixture of both

In the bowl of the food processor, process the mustard, eggs, salt, and lemon juice. With the motor running, add ½ cup of the oil mixture, one drop at a time. Once the mixture begins to thicken, add the remaining oil in a thin stream.

YIELD: ABOUT 2½ CUPS

BASIC MAYONNAISE

There is nothing like a bowl of homemade mayonnaise. No commercial product can replace the tartly delicious flavor of this sauce when it is freshly made. Not only is this classic mixture necessary for many salads and sandwiches, it is also the basis of many complicated, more sophisticated sauces. It isn't difficult to make, however, and you will want to prepare it often.

> 2 *large egg yolks*
> 1 *teaspoon Dijon mustard*
> 1 *teaspoon fresh lemon juice*
> *Salt and freshly ground black pepper to taste*
> 1 *cup olive oil or vegetable oil or a mixture of both*

In a medium-size mixing bowl, beat together the egg yolks, mustard, lemon juice, salt, and pepper with a whisk. Whisk in the oil, a few drops at a time, until the mixture thickens and begins to look like mayonnaise. Then beat in the remaining oil in a thin stream. Add a little more lemon juice if the mixture is too thick. Serve at room temperature.

YIELD: ABOUT 1 CUP

❧ BASIL MAYONNAISE

Freshly caught fish—steamed, poached, or grilled—will never be better than when accompanied by this sauce. Or, serve it with an onion and tomato salad for a true summer delight.

> 1 *cup Basic Mayonnaise (above)*
> 1 *cup fresh basil leaves, very finely chopped*
> 1 *bunch scallions, white part only, minced*

Beat together all the ingredients in a medium-size mixing bowl. Chill several hours to develop the flavors before serving. Serve at room temperature.

YIELD: ABOUT 1½ CUPS

❧ COLD CURRY MAYONNAISE

There is no reason to confine the delicious taste of curry to hot dishes. This fragrant cold sauce is a perfect summer accompaniment for cold poached fish, fish or chicken salad, or even cold roasted lamb.

> *½ cup Basic Mayonnaise (page 68)*
> *2 tablespoons fresh lemon juice*
> *¼ cup clam juice*
> *2 tablespoons hot curry powder*
> *Salt and freshly ground black pepper to taste*

Beat together all the ingredients in a small mixing bowl. Let the mixture stand, refrigerated, at least one hour before serving to develop the flavors.

YIELD: ABOUT ¾ CUP

❧ CRAB SAUCE

This unusual sauce can also be used as a dip for crudités or a spread for crackers. It is sensational with cold boiled potatoes, hard-boiled eggs, artichoke hearts, or cold, steamed shellfish.

> *2 tablespoons white wine vinegar*
> *1 cup Basic Mayonnaise (page 68)*
> *1 tablespoon Dijon mustard*
> *2 tablespoons fresh lemon juice*
> *2 cloves garlic, minced*
> *1 scallion, white and light green parts only, minced*
> *1 teaspoon soy sauce*
> *½ cup flaked crab meat (do not use lump crabmeat)*
> *Salt and freshly ground pepper*

In a medium-size mixing bowl, beat the vinegar into the mayonnaise. Then whisk in the mustard, lemon juice, garlic, and scallion. Stir in the soy sauce and crabmeat and season well with salt and pepper. Serve at room temperature.

YIELD: ABOUT 1½ CUPS

❧ CUCUMBER SAUCE

Cucumbers are not only crisp and refreshing, but they are also high in vitamin C, as long as they are not peeled. Once the seeds are removed, the majority of people are not bothered by the gastric distress that whole cucumbers can sometimes produce. The crunch they add to this sauce makes it an intriguing accompaniment for poached fish or cold roasted lamb.

> *¹⁄₄ cup Basic Mayonnaise (page 68)*
> *¹⁄₄ cup plain yogurt*
> *¹⁄₃ cup finely diced seeded cucumber*
> *1 tablespoon minced scallion, white and light green parts only*
> *1 tablespoon chopped fresh dill*

Stir together all the ingredients in a small mixing bowl and chill for several hours before serving.

YIELD: ABOUT ²⁄₃ CUP

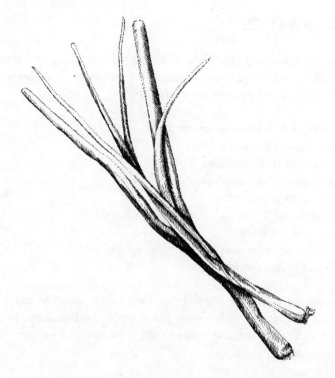

❧ GARLIC CREAM

This thinner sauce does not have the impact that aioli does, but it is still very pungent. True garlic lovers should be in heaven when this is served. It is spectacular with cold steamed lobster. Serve it over poached fish, too.

For those who are less adventurous, simmering the garlic in water tends to remove most of its offensive strength.

> 8 cloves garlic, peeled, simmered over low heat in enough water to cover for 15 minutes, and drained
> 2 tablespoons white wine vinegar
> 1/2 cup Basic Mayonnaise (page 68)
> 1/2 cup sour cream
> Salt and freshly ground black pepper to taste
> 2 tablespoons chopped fresh parsley

Puree the garlic in a blender or with a mortar and pestle. Transfer it to a medium-size bowl and whisk in the vinegar. Then stir in the mayonnaise and sour cream. Season well with salt and pepper, stir in the parsley, and serve.

YIELD: ABOUT 1 CUP

❧ GINGER LIME MAYONNAISE

Bring a little touch of the Caribbean to your meal with this delightfully different sauce. Serve it with fruit, cold roast pork, and salads of all kinds.

> 1/2 cup Basic Mayonnaise (page 68)
> 1/2 cup plain yogurt
> 1 tablespoon grated lime zest
> 3 tablespoons fresh lime juice
> 1 tablespoon grated fresh ginger
> 2 tablespoons honey

Beat together all the ingredients in a small bowl. Chill several hours before serving.

YIELD: ABOUT 1 CUP

❧ GOAT CHEESE DRESSING

The tart flavor of goat cheese makes this an especially refreshing dressing for green salads.

1/4 pound fresh goat cheese (Boucheron, Montrachet, etc.), cut into chunks
1/2 cup Basic Mayonnaise (page 68)
1 clove garlic, minced
2 tablespoons heavy cream
2 tablespoons chopped fresh parsley
Salt and freshly ground black pepper to taste

Place all the ingredients in a blender or small food processor and blend until smooth. Serve at room temperature.

YIELD: ABOUT 1 CUP

❧ GREEN GODDESS DRESSING

Named after a popular play, this delicious dressing was developed at the Palace Hotel in San Francisco during the 1920s. The salty taste of the anchovies makes this sauce a perfect foil for cold seafood, or for green or mixed salads. Note that you can experiment by using different vinegars—white wine, cider, even red wine—to achieve different tastes and colors.

1 cup Basic Mayonnaise (page 68)
3 anchovy fillets, chopped
1 scallion, white and light green parts only, minced
2 tablespoons fresh lemon juice
3 tablespoons chopped fresh parsley
2 tablespoons vinegar

Whisk together all the ingredients in a small bowl and chill several hours before serving. Serve chilled.

YIELD: ABOUT 1 1/2 CUPS

❧ GREEN MAYONNAISE

This mayonnaise contains so many herbs that it takes on a lovely pale green color. Serve it with cold steamed shellfish, fish, and all sorts of vegetables, steamed or raw.

> 1 cup chopped watercress
> 1 cup chopped fresh parsley
> 1 bunch scallions, white and light green parts only, minced
> 1 large clove garlic, minced (or more, to taste)
> 1 tablespoon chopped fresh rosemary
> 1 tablespoon chopped fresh oregano
> 1 cup Basic Mayonnaise (page 68)

Beat all the ingredients together in a medium-size mixing bowl. Chill several hours or overnight to allow the flavors to develop before serving. Serve chilled.

YIELD: ABOUT 2 CUPS

❧ HORSERADISH DILL SAUCE

Oh, the joys of summer—and this sauce is certainly one of them. Use it when you grill meat, fish, or vegetables, or to top a fresh salad.

> 1/3 cup grated fresh horseradish
> 1/3 cup white wine vinegar
> 1/4 cup minced dill pickle
> 1/3 cup Basic Mayonnaise (page 68)
> 1/2 cup plain yogurt
> 1 tablespoon chopped fresh dill
> Salt and freshly ground black pepper to taste

Combine all the ingredients in a medium-size mixing bowl. Chill, covered, for several hours or overnight. Return to room temperature before serving.

YIELD: ABOUT 2 CUPS

✷ LEMON MAYONNAISE

The refreshing citrus flavor makes this mayonnaise terrific for cold meat
or cheese sandwiches. Serve it with hot or cold steamed fish, and don't
miss it with cold roast chicken.

> 1 cup Basic Mayonnaise (page 68)
> 5 tablespoons grated lemon zest
> 5 tablespoons fresh lemon juice
> Salt and freshly ground black pepper to taste

Whisk together all the ingredients in a small mixing bowl. Chill for
several hours before serving. Serve chilled or at room temperature.
     YIELD: ABOUT 1 CUP

✷ LOUIS DRESSING

There are some conflicting accounts about the origin of this sauce, which
is customarily served with crabmeat. Most likely it was developed in
Seattle, Washington, where it is said that it became a favorite of Enrico
Caruso during one of his tours to that part of our country. Try this with
any seafood, especially shrimp or lobster, or cold poultry.

> 1 cup Basic Mayonnaise (page 68)
> 1/2 cup good quality chili sauce
> 1/2 small onion, minced
> 1/3 cup heavy cream, whipped to stiff peaks
> Red (cayenne) pepper to taste
> 1 tablespoon chopped fresh parsley

Beat together all the ingredients until smooth. Chill several hours before
serving. Return to room temperature before serving.
     YIELD: ABOUT 2 CUPS

❧ MACHINE MINT MAYONNAISE

For those summer parties when quantity is a necessity, try this version of
my hand-made mixture.

> 1 tablespoon Dijon mustard
> 3 large eggs
> ½ teaspoon salt
> 2 tablespoons homemade (page 175) or commercial Mint Sauce
> 1½ to 2 cups vegetable oil
> 1 cup fresh mint leaves, chopped

In the bowl of the food processor, process the mustard, eggs, salt, and
mint sauce until smooth. With the motor running, add ½ cup oil, one
drop at a time. When the mixture thickens, add the remaining oil in a thin
stream. Once all the oil has been incorporated, pour the mayonnaise into
a bowl and beat in the chopped mint. Can be served at room temperature
or chilled.

YIELD: ABOUT 3 CUPS

❧ MINT GREEN SAUCE

Similar in color to Green Mayonnaise (page 73), this aromatic sauce
combines the two related flavors of basil and mint, which will enhance any
cold roasted or grilled meat, especially lamb. You can also team it with
cold poached salmon, trout, or bluefish.

> 2 cloves garlic, finely minced
> ½ cup chopped fresh basil
> 3 tablespoons chopped fresh mint
> 1 cup Basic Mayonnaise (page 68)

Beat the garlic and herbs into the mayonnaise. Chill for several hours
before serving. Serve at room temperature.

YIELD: ABOUT 1½ CUPS

❦ MINT MAYONNAISE

The sharp taste of the mint sauce in this mayonnaise makes it a great accompaniment for cold fish, but especially with warm grilled vegetables. Try it with crudités, too.

> 2 tablespoons homemade (page 175) or commercial Mint Sauce
> 1 teaspoon Dijon mustard
> 2 large egg yolks
> Salt and freshly ground black pepper to taste
> 1 cup olive or vegetable oil
> 1 cup fresh mint leaves, chopped

Beat together the mint sauce, mustard, egg yolks, salt, and pepper in a medium-size mixing bowl. Beat in the oil, a few drops at a time, until the mixture is thickened, then whisk in the remaining oil in a thin stream. Stir in the mint. Chill several hours to allow the flavors to develop, but let warm to room temperature before serving.

YIELD: ABOUT 1½ CUPS

❧ RAVIGOTE SAUCE

This is the cold version of this flavorful sauce (you'll find the hot version on page 42). As a summer accompaniment for cold meats and fish, it is extraordinary. Head cheese, even garlicky sausage, goes very well with it, too. Try it with steamed or poached vegetables, or use it the next time you serve a crudité platter.

1 large hard-boiled egg yolk
2 tablespoons tarragon vinegar
⅓ cup olive oil
2 large shallots, minced, blanched 1 minute in boiling water and drained
1 tablespoon Dijon mustard
1 teaspoon chopped fresh chervil
1 teaspoon chopped fresh tarragon
1 teaspoon chopped fresh chives
2 tablespoons chopped fresh parsley
Salt and freshly ground black pepper to taste

In a small mixing bowl, mash the egg yolk into the vinegar with a fork to form a smooth paste. Beat in all the oil a little at a time until the mixture is as thick as mayonnaise. Beat in the shallots, mustard, and herbs, and season to taste with salt and pepper. Chill several hours to develop the flavors. Serve chilled.

YIELD: ABOUT ⅔ CUP

❧ RED PEPPER MAYONNAISE

Anyone who likes sweet peppers will love this sauce. Serve it with grilled fish for a deliciously different dish.

For a quick sauce, stir the catsup and red pepper into 1 cup home-made or commercial mayonnaise. Let the mixture stand 30 minutes before serving.

> *1 large egg yolk*
> *1 teaspoon prepared mustard*
> *1 tablespoon fresh lemon juice*
> *1 cup olive oil*
> *3 tablespoons catsup*
> *1 sweet red bell pepper, roasted (page 155), peeled, seeded, and diced*

Beat the egg yolk, mustard, and lemon juice together in a small mixing bowl. Whisk in all the oil a little at a time, until the mixture thickens. Beat in the remaining oil in a steady stream, then add the catsup and pepper. Serve at room temperature.

YIELD: ABOUT 1 ½ CUPS

❧ REMOULADE SAUCE

In the South, this sauce is frequently served with fried fish or shellfish. It is a sharp, delicious mayonnaise that also goes well with cold fish or shellfish, and even cold roast poultry.

> *½ cup finely chopped cornichons or sour pickles*
> *2 tablespoons capers, chopped*
> *1 tablespoon Dijon mustard*
> *1 teaspoon chopped fresh tarragon*
> *1 tablespoon chopped fresh chervil*
> *¼ cup chopped fresh parsley*
> *2 cups Basic Mayonnaise (page 68)*

Dry the cornichons and capers on paper towels. Transfer them to a medium-size mixing bowl and add the mustard and herbs. Stir in the mayonnaise, then chill for several hours. Beat well and return to room temperature before serving.

YIELD: ABOUT 2 ½ CUPS

❧ ROUILLE

In French *rouille* means rust. It's uncertain if that is what too much of this very powerful sauce does to your insides, but it is a clear description of the lovely color it takes on.

Traditionally, rouille is served with bouillabaise or other hearty fish soups. It is either spread on toast rounds, which are floated in the soup, or spooned, gingerly, directly into the soup and stirred to mix. Care should be taken that guests know exactly how hot this sauce really is.

½ cup fresh soft white bread crumbs
¼ cup Fish Stock (page 13) or dry white wine
2 small hot red chilies, stemmed and seeded (or 1 teaspoon crushed red pepper
*   or 2 small dried red peppers, softened in boiling water and drained)*
3 to 4 cloves garlic, minced
2 large egg yolks
¼ cup olive oil

In a small bowl, soak the bread crumbs in the fish stock or dry white wine for 10 minutes, then squeeze dry with your hands. Then, puree the chilies, garlic, egg yolks, and bread in the bowl of a food processor to make a smooth paste. With the processor running, add the oil in a thin stream through the feed tube. The sauce should thicken and be the consistency of mayonnaise. If it is too thick, beat in a little cold fish stock, one tablespoon at a time. Serve at room temperature.

YIELD: ABOUT ⅔ CUP

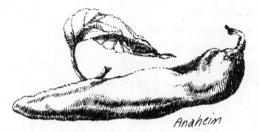

Anaheim

❧ RUSSIAN DRESSING

Frequently this flavorful sauce is served only with salads or sandwiches. Try it as an accompaniment for cold shellfish, or cold poached fish such as salmon or bluefish.

> 1/4 cup good quality chili sauce
> 1 teaspoon minced pimiento
> 2 tablespoons finely chopped fresh chives
> 1 cup Basic Mayonnaise (page 68)

Mix together all the ingredients. Chill several hours to allow flavors to develop. Serve chilled.

YIELD: ABOUT 1 1/4 CUPS

❧ SAUCE GRIBICHE

Here is a chunky, refreshing, classic French sauce that perks up cold poached fish.

> 3 large hard-boiled eggs, peeled, the whites diced, and yolks set aside
> 1 tablespoon Dijon mustard
> 1/2 cup peanut oil
> 2 tablespoons chopped fresh parsley
> 1 teaspoon capers, chopped
> 2 cornichons (or small sour gherkins), chopped
> 2 tablespoons chopped fresh chervil
> 2 tablespoons chopped fresh tarragon
> Salt and freshly ground black pepper to taste

Mash the egg yolks in a small mixing bowl with a fork, then beat in the mustard. Using a whisk, beat in the oil a little at a time until the mixture is thick, then beat in the remaining oil in a steady stream. Stir in the remaining ingredients and season well with salt and pepper. Chill several hours to develop the flavors. Serve chilled.

YIELD: ABOUT 1 CUP

🎋 SOUTH OF THE BORDER MAYONNAISE

There is a definite Mexican flavor to this delicious mayonnaise sauce. Serve it with hot or cold poached or grilled fish or with grilled chicken or steak.

> 2 jalapeño peppers, seeded and minced (be careful not to burn hands or eyes)
> 2 tablespoons chopped fresh coriander (cilantro)
> 1 teaspoon finely chopped fresh Mexican oregano or 2 teaspoons regular oregano
> ½ cup Basic Mayonnaise (page 68)

Puree the peppers, coriander, and oregano in a blender or food processor. Beat the puree into the mayonnaise and chill for several hours to allow the flavors to develop. Return to room temperature before serving.

YIELD: ABOUT ¾ CUP

🎋 SUN-DRIED TOMATO MAYONNAISE

Sun-dried tomatoes became quite the rage several years ago, and, as with all gastronomic trends, were greatly overused. But this method of incorporating their unique flavor deserves to be preserved. Serve this mayonnaise with cold cuts, cold roasted meats, cold poached fish, or salads.

> 6 to 8 sun-dried tomatoes (not oil-packed, if possible)
> ¼ teaspoon saffron, soaked in 1 teaspoon hot water for 5 minutes
> 1 clove garlic, minced
> 1 cup Basic Mayonnaise (page 68)
> 1 tablespoon chopped fresh parsley
> Salt to taste

Reconstitute the dry tomatoes in hot, but not boiling water for five minutes. Drain and dry them. If using oil-packed tomatoes, blot all the excess oil with paper towels. Chop the tomatoes.

Beat all the ingredients together and season well with salt. Let the mixture stand for one hour; beat well before serving. Serve at room temperature.

YIELD: ABOUT 1¼ CUPS

❦ TAPENADE MAYONNAISE

Tapenade is an olive and anchovy mixture from the south of France that is traditionally spread on little rounds of toasted bread and eaten while drinking the local wines. Its salty goodness tends to increase the consumption of the beverage. Mixed with homemade mayonnaise, tapenade creates a delightful sauce for cold roasted veal, poached poultry, or grilled fish.

1 cup Basic Mayonnaise (page 68)
1 cup oil-cured olives, pitted and minced
6 anchovy fillets, rinsed, dried, and minced
3 cloves garlic, minced
2 tablespoons fresh lemon juice
1/4 cup minced fresh parsley

Beat together all the ingredients. Chill several hours or overnight to allow the flavors to develop. Return to room temperature and beat well before serving.

YIELD: ABOUT 1 1/2 CUPS

❦ TARRAGON CREAM DRESSING

Tarragon adds a slight anise taste to this delightful sauce that goes very well with hot vegetables, crudités, mixed green salads, vegetable salads, and cold seafood.

1/2 cup sour cream or plain yogurt
1/2 cup Basic Mayonnaise (page 68)
2 tablespoons Dijon mustard
3 tablespoons chopped fresh tarragon
1 clove garlic, minced
Salt and freshly ground black pepper to taste

Beat together all the ingredients and season well with salt and pepper. Chill an hour or more before serving. Serve chilled.

YIELD: ABOUT 1 1/2 CUPS

✿ TARTARE SAUCE

Generally this sauce is served with fried fish or shellfish. In the South, it is the classic accompaniment to fried oysters, fried catfish, or fried shrimp. Many people like it with any fish or shellfish, whether poached or steamed, hot or cold. The pungent taste of onion, pickle, and capers makes a great contrast to mild-flavored fish, and the acidity tends to cut the greasy feel of fried foods. For a more rustic sauce, don't chop the onion and pickle too finely. Make plenty—you'll find people really like this.

> 1 cup Basic Mayonnaise (page 68)
> 1 tablespoon chopped fresh tarragon
> 2 tablespoons chopped fresh parsley
> 2 tablespoons heavy cream (optional)
> 2 tablespoons dry white wine
> 1 to 2 tablespoons finely minced onion or scallion
> 1 tablespoon capers, drained and chopped
> 2 to 3 tablespoons chopped dill pickle or cornichons
> Salt and freshly ground black pepper to taste

Thoroughly combine all the ingredients. Chill several hours before serving. Serve chilled.

YIELD: ABOUT 2 CUPS

❧ THOUSAND ISLAND DRESSING

Presumably named for the "islands" created by the chunky ingredients, this sauce may have been developed for the opening of the Blackstone Hotel in Chicago in the early 1900s. It is traditionally served with wedges of crisp iceberg lettuce, but goes equally well with other salads, cold shellfish, or as an accompaniment for crudités.

> 3 tablespoons good quality chili sauce
> 1/2 teaspoon Worcestershire sauce
> 1 medium-size, ripe tomato, peeled, seeded, and chopped
> 1 teaspoon chopped pimiento
> 2 tablespoons chopped fresh parsley
> 1 tablespoon minced green bell pepper
> 1 cup Basic Mayonnaise (page 68)
> 1 large hard-boiled egg, peeled and chopped

Beat together all the ingredients. Chill several hours and beat well before serving. Serve chilled.

YIELD: ABOUT 1 1/2 CUPS

❧ TOMATO BASIL MAYONNAISE

Make this sauce in midsummer when tomatoes are full of flavor and basil is going wild in the sun. It will make your salads something special and should be on every summer buffet along with cold meats and cold poached or grilled fish of all kinds.

> 1 cup Basic Mayonnaise (page 68), made with all olive oil
> 1 large, ripe tomato, peeled, seeded, and finely chopped
> 1 tablespoon fresh lime juice
> 3 tablespoons chopped fresh basil
> 2 scallions, white and light green parts only, minced

Combine thoroughly all the ingredients in a small bowl. Chill several hours to allow the flavors to develop. Allow to return to room temperature and stir well before serving.

YIELD: ABOUT 1 1/2 CUPS

❧ TUNA SAUCE

Often this sauce is served with cold roasted veal in the classic Italian summer dish of vitello tonnato. The sauce is generally made with a little veal stock, causing it to gel slightly when chilled—making it the perfect covering for cold meats. This version is a little thicker, but goes equally well with cold veal or turkey. You can serve it with hard-boiled eggs and tomatoes, too.

One 10-ounce can oil-packed tuna, drained
6 anchovy fillets
1 teaspoon capers
¼ cup fresh lemon juice
⅔ cup olive oil
Salt and freshly ground black pepper to taste

Puree the tuna, anchovies, and capers in a food processor. Add the lemon juice and pulse until mixed. With the processor running, add all the oil, a little at a time, through the feed tube until the sauce is thick. Season well with salt and pepper. May be served at once or chilled for several hours.

YIELD: ABOUT 1½ CUPS

❧ WALNUT MAYONNAISE

The unique flavor of this sauce makes it perfect for grilled fish or poultry. If walnuts are a little too strong for your taste, make the sauce with pecans instead.

> *½ cup walnuts halves or pieces*
> *Freshly ground black pepper to taste*
> *1 cup Basic Mayonnaise (page 68), made with a combination of ⅓ cup*
>   *walnut oil and ⅔ cup extra-virgin olive oil*

Preheat the oven to 475°F. Spread the walnuts on a baking sheet and toast them for 4 to 5 minutes, watching constantly to see that they do not burn and stirring from time to time. Cool completely and chop finely.

   Beat the pepper and walnuts into the mayonnaise. Chill at least one hour and remove from the refrigerator 15 minutes before serving.

   YIELD: ABOUT 1½ CUPS

CHAPTER SEVEN

❧ *Compound Butters*

COMPOUND BUTTERS ARE A COOK'S LIFESAVER. THESE SAVORY OR SWEET mixtures can be prepared whenever the mood strikes. They keep well in the refrigerator for one week and in the freezer for three months. A whole collection in the freezer provides an instant supply of sauces.

In fact, my friend Nika Hazelton once pointed out that many of the savory compound butters make outstanding pasta sauces. Toss cooked pasta of any kind with several tablespoons of one of these butters, serve with a green salad and lots of crusty bread, and you have a meal that can be prepared in literally just a few minutes.

Many chefs insist on unsalted butter for all compound butters, but I only use it for some sweet varieties. Much sweet butter in the United States has a slightly sour taste that I find unappealing and since many of these mixtures call for adding a little salt, I simply start with a high quality salted butter.

Sweet compound butters add something extra special to breakfast breads and muffins, and are really delicious when spread on waffles, pancakes, or French toast. Garlic and herb butters are equally delicious with homemade bread for lunch or dinner.

Beat the butter in a bowl until it is light and fluffy and then beat in the additional ingredients. Almost any ingredient can be incorporated into the softened butter. While this book provides a generous selection of ideas, don't forget to use your own imagination and combine it with the ingredients you have on hand.

COMPOUND BUTTER TIPS

- Soften the butter to be used at room temperature until it can be easily stirred with a wooden spoon. Do not soften it in the oven, in a microwave, or on top of the stove.

● When mixing the butter together with the other ingredients, *do not* use a food processor or blender, or the compound butter will lose all of its texture.

❧ ALMOND BUTTER

A slice of this brings out a special flavor in grilled poultry. Of course, it also goes well with hot muffins, waffles, pancakes, and French toast.

½ cup almonds
¼ pound (1 stick) butter, softened

Blanch the almonds in boiling water for 3 minutes, then drain and rub them dry with a cloth dish towel to remove the dark skin. Place the almonds in a food processor and pulse several times to chop the almonds finely, but do not puree them.

Transfer the almonds to a small bowl and cream them with the butter. Do not use the food processor to mix the butter and almonds.

Form the mixture into a cylinder, wrap it in waxed paper, and chill until ready to use.

YIELD: ABOUT ½ CUP

❧ COLD ANCHOVY BUTTER

This is a great combination for topping grilled or steamed fish.

4 anchovy fillets
¼ pound (1 stick) butter, softened

Rinse the anchovy fillets and dry them on paper towels. In a bowl, mash the fillets with a fork until they are reduced to a paste. Then cream the anchovy paste with the butter. Form the mixture into a cylinder, wrap in waxed paper, and chill until ready to use.

YIELD: ABOUT ½ CUP

❧ AVOCADO BUTTER

A little of this butter on steamed vegetables, grilled tomatoes, or broiled fish will turn a simple dish into something special.

1 large, ripe avocado, peeled, stoned, and pureed
1 tablespoon fresh lemon juice
½ pound (2 sticks) butter, softened
1 teaspoon minced onion
3 tablespoons chopped fresh parsley
1 tablespoon chopped fresh basil
Salt to taste
Hot pepper sauce to taste

Beat together all the ingredients in a large mixing bowl; do not use a food processor or blender. Shape the avocado butter into a cylinder, wrap in waxed paper, and chill until ready to use.

YIELD: ABOUT 1 CUP

❧ BERCY BUTTER

Top a grilled steak, veal chop, or double thick pork chop with a slice of this butter for a full-flavored treat. You can also make this with red wine and call it Marchand de Vin Butter.

2 teaspoons finely chopped shallots
½ cup dry white wine
1 teaspoon fresh lemon juice
4 tablespoons (½ stick) butter, softened
2 teaspoons chopped fresh parsley
Salt and freshly ground black pepper to taste

In a small, heavy saucepan over medium heat, cook the shallots in the white wine and lemon juice until almost all the liquid has evaporated. Cool completely.

Cream the cooled shallot mixture with the butter, parsley, and seasonings in a small bowl. Form the mixture into a cylinder, wrap in waxed paper, and chill until ready to use.

YIELD: ABOUT ⅓ CUP

✢ BLACK PEPPER BUTTER

A little of this will add a lot of zing to plain grilled fish and meat.

> *¼ pound (1 stick) butter, softened*
> *1 tablespoon coarsely ground black pepper*

Cream the pepper into the butter in a small bowl. Form the mixture into a cylinder, wrap in waxed paper, and chill until ready to use.

YIELD: ABOUT ½ CUP

✢ BLUE CHEESE BRANDY BUTTER

While this is an excellent accompaniment for both beef and lamb, it is also very good as a spread for pumpernickel bread. You can also serve it on crackers as a snack with cocktails.

> *¼ pound (1 stick) butter, softened*
> *⅓ cup crumbled blue cheese*
> *½ cup chopped fresh parsley*
> *2 tablespoons brandy*
> *1 small clove garlic, minced*
> *Freshly ground black pepper to taste*

Cream together all the ingredients in a small bowl. Form the mixture into a cylinder, wrap in waxed paper, and chill until ready to use.

YIELD: ABOUT 1 CUP

❧ CARLTON BUTTER

The combination of Worcestershire sauce and chutney makes this a deliciously pungent addition to grilled fish and poultry.

1/4 pound (1 stick) butter, softened
1 teaspoon Worcestershire sauce
2 teaspoons mango or Peach Chutney (page 224), finely chopped
2 tablespoons good quality chili sauce (or Fresh Tomato Sauce, page 122)

Cream together all the ingredients in a small bowl. Form the mixture into a cylinder, wrap in waxed paper, and chill until ready to use.

YIELD: ABOUT 1/2 CUP

❧ GARLIC BASIL BUTTER

Toss some of this with your favorite pasta, make a tomato salad and open a bottle of wine. Dinner is ready.

1/2 cup chopped fresh basil
3 cloves garlic, minced
1/4 pound (1 stick) butter, softened
Freshly ground black pepper to taste

Beat together all the ingredients in a small bowl. Form the mixture into a cylinder, wrap in waxed paper, and chill until ready to use.

YIELD: ABOUT 1/2 CUP

❧ GARLIC BUTTER

Spread this tangy mixture on Italian bread and run it under the broiler until it bubbles. Or use it to top a grilled steak, a slab of tuna, or freshly steamed green beans. This is truly an all-purpose spread.

>   *3 cloves garlic, finely chopped*
>   *1/4 pound (1 stick) butter*
>   *2 tablespoons fresh lemon juice*
>   *2 tablespoons chopped fresh parsley*
>   *Salt and freshly ground black pepper to taste*

In a mortar, with a pestle, mash the garlic into a paste. Beat the garlic into the butter, then add the lemon juice and parsley. Season well with salt and pepper. Form the mixture into a cylinder, wrap in waxed paper, and chill until ready to use.

YIELD: ABOUT 1/2 CUP

❧ GARLIC BUTTER II

This is a very hearty spread, not for the fainthearted. True garlic lovers will enjoy every lingering taste. Try it on grilled shellfish.

>   *6 cloves garlic, peeled and blanched in boiling water for 6 minutes*
>   *1/4 pound (1 stick) butter, softened*
>   *2 tablespoons chopped fresh parsley*

Puree the blanched garlic in a food processor by dropping the cloves one at a time into the feed tube while the processor is running. Then cream the puree with the softened butter in a small bowl and beat in the parsley. Form the mixture into a cylinder, wrap in waxed paper, and chill until ready to use.

YIELD: ABOUT 1/2 CUP

🐝 GORGONZOLA BUTTER

Spread this on French bread, broil until bubbly, and serve with grilled steak. Or simply top the steak with a slice. The hearty flavor of the Gorgonzola cheese also goes well with grilled pork chops. And you will want to keep some on hand to toss with steamed or grilled vegetables, as well.

> *¹/₄ pound (1 stick) butter, softened*
> *3 tablespoons Gorgonzola cheese, at room temperature*

Cream the butter with the softened cheese. Form the mixture into a cylinder, wrap in waxed paper, and chill until ready to use.

YIELD: ABOUT ½ CUP

🐝 GREEN PEPPERCORN BUTTER

Green peppercorns add aroma and flavor to this butter without the sharp bite of dried pepper. Spread a small amount over a grilled or broiled steak, or use it as a seasoning for steamed summer squash.

> *¹/₄ pound (1 stick) butter, softened*
> *Salt and freshly ground black pepper to taste*
> *2 tablespoons Dijon mustard*
> *1 tablespoon chopped fresh parsley*
> *1 tablespoon minced onion*
> *2 teaspoons green peppercorns, chopped*
> *1 teaspoon brandy*

Cream together all the ingredients in a small bowl. Form the mixture into a cylinder, wrap in waxed paper, and chill until ready to use.

YIELD: ABOUT ½ CUP

❧ HERB BUTTER

Homemade breads and savory muffins are even better when served with this butter combination. In fact, it goes with nearly everything: meats, poultry, fish, pasta of all kinds, fresh vegetables. Try a slice on a fluffy baked potato.

> *2 tablespoons chopped fresh parsley*
> *1 teaspoon chopped fresh chervil*
> *1 teaspoon chopped fresh tarragon*
> *6 spinach leaves, rinsed thoroughly, dried, and finely chopped*
> *2 large shallots, minced*
> *¼ pound (1 stick) butter, softened*

Cream together all the ingredients in a small bowl. Form the mixture into a cylinder, wrap in waxed paper, and chill until ready to use.

YIELD: ABOUT ½ CUP

❧ LIME AND PEPPER BUTTER

Piquant and refreshing, this butter is wonderful on grilled fish steaks as well as roasted, baked, or grilled poultry.

> *¼ pound (1 stick) butter, softened*
> *1 teaspoon grated lime zest*
> *2 tablespoons fresh lime juice*
> *1½ tablespoons chopped fresh coriander (cilantro)*
> *½ teaspoon crushed red pepper*

Beat together all the ingredients in a small bowl. Form the mixture into a cylinder, wrap in waxed paper, and chill until ready to use.

YIELD: ABOUT ½ CUP

❧ LIME BUTTER

Grilled fish never had it so good! A slice of this on a thick swordfish steak is all the seasoning it needs. You can also serve it with any green vegetable. It is especially good with steamed carrots or fresh asparagus.

¼ pound (1 stick) butter, softened
2 tablespoons fresh lime juice
1 tablespoon freshly grated lime zest
2 tablespoons soy sauce

Cream together all the ingredients in a small bowl. Form the mixture into a cylinder, wrap in waxed paper, and chill until ready to use.

YIELD: ABOUT ½ CUP

❧ MAÎTRE D'HÔTEL BUTTER

Keep this butter on hand and you'll always have an instant condiment for grilled fish and meat. It is also delightful with steamed vegetables such as broccoli, asparagus, even artichokes.

¼ pound (1 stick) butter, softened
1 tablespoon chopped fresh parsley
1 tablespoon fresh lemon juice
Salt and freshly ground black pepper to taste

Beat together all ingredients in a small bowl. Form the mixture into a cylinder, wrap in waxed paper, and chill until ready to use.

YIELD: ABOUT ½ CUP

❧ MUSTARD SHALLOT BUTTER

Who can resist a charcoal-grilled steak with a touch of this tangy mustard-flavored butter? Serve it with fish, vegetables, and poultry, too.

¼ pound (1 stick) butter, softened
2 tablespoons Dijon mustard
1 large shallot, minced
Salt and freshly ground black pepper to taste
¼ cup chopped fresh parsley

Beat together all the ingredients. Form the mixture into a cylinder, wrap in waxed paper, and chill until ready to use.

YIELD: ABOUT ½ CUP

❧ ORANGE BUTTER

When cold, this sweet butter is wonderful with breakfast muffins, pancakes, waffles, or French toast. After dinner, it's perfect melted on top of ice cream or a crepe suzette.

¼ pound (1 stick) butter, softened
2 tablespoons Grand Marnier or other orange liqueur
2 tablespoons grated orange zest

Cream together all the ingredients until smooth in a small bowl. Form into a log and roll in waxed paper. Chill until ready to serve.

YIELD: ABOUT ½ CUP

🦐 SHALLOT BUTTER

This is another delicious accompaniment for broiled or charcoal-grilled beef, pork, poultry, and fish. It is equally delicious with many vegetables, including baked or roasted potatoes.

> 2 tablespoons finely minced shallots, blanched in boiling water for 3 minutes, and then drained
> 1/4 pound (1 stick) butter, softened
> 2 tablespoons chopped fresh parsley

Cream all the ingredients together in a small bowl. Form the mixture into a cylinder, wrap in waxed paper, and chill until ready to use.

YIELD: ABOUT 1/2 CUP

🦐 SHRIMP BUTTER

This is an essential ingredient in Sauce Nantua (page 44), a more sophisticated combination, but you can use it with grilled, steamed, or poached seafood as well.

> 10 large precooked shrimp, shelled
> 12 tablespoons (1 1/2 sticks) butter, softened
> Salt and freshly ground black pepper to taste
> 1 tablespoon chopped fresh parsley

Chop (but do not puree) the shrimp in a food processor or by hand. Beat into the softened butter with a wooden spoon. Season well with salt and pepper and cream in the parsley. Form the mixture into a cylinder, wrap in waxed paper, and chill until ready to use.

YIELD: ABOUT 1 CUP

❧ SMOKED SALMON BUTTER

Try this on toasted bagels, or use it to top grilled fish or shellfish. Add
a little chopped parsley, if desired.

> *¼ pound (1 stick) butter, softened*
> *2 ounces smoked salmon, chopped*

Beat the butter with the salmon in a small bowl until smooth. Do not use
the food processor to mix the butter and salmon. Form the mixture into
a cylinder, wrap in waxed paper, and chill until ready to use.

YIELD: ABOUT ½ CUP

❧ SNAIL BUTTER

This is perhaps the most classic of all composed butters—totally delicious
with snails, other shellfish, French bread, and many freshly steamed or
simmered vegetables. If garlic is your passion, add a little more.

> *¼ pound (1 stick) butter, softened*
> *1 large shallot, finely minced*
> *2 cloves garlic, finely minced*
> *2 tablespoons brandy*
> *1 tablespoon chopped fresh parsley*
> *Salt and freshly ground black pepper to taste*

Cream together all the ingredients in a small bowl. Form the mixture into
a cylinder, wrap in waxed paper, and chill until ready to use.

YIELD: ABOUT ½ CUP

❧ SUN-DRIED TOMATO AND BASIL BUTTER

Toss this with any kind of pasta for an instant sauce. Or use it to flavor freshly steamed vegetables or a grilled chicken breast.

> 1/4 pound (1 stick) butter, softened
> 1/4 cup oil-packed sun-dried tomatoes, drained and minced
> 1 clove garlic, minced
> Freshly ground black pepper to taste
> 1/2 cup chopped fresh basil

Beat together all the ingredients in a small bowl. Form the mixture into a cylinder, wrap in waxed paper, and chill until ready to use.

YIELD: ABOUT 3/4 CUP

CHAPTER EIGHT

❧ *Marinades and Barbecue Sauces*

OUTDOOR COOKS ARE CONSTANTLY ON THE LOOKOUT FOR THE PERFECT MARI-nade or are always experimenting to produce their own distinctive barbe-cue sauce. It seems to be a passion that goes along with a love of the smoky flavor imparted by grilling over charcoal or hardwood fires.

I have provided a large selection of both types of sauces and hope that you will enjoy them, and then expand upon them, possibly to find the one that will become an essential part of your outdoor cooking.

Marinades are generally thin and contain some acidic element—wine, lemon or lime juice, or vinegar—that acts to slightly tenderize the meat or fish. Some type of oil is usually another component. As the acid breaks down the fiber of the meat, the oil penetrates it, making the cooked food more moist and succulent. Marinades are generally highly flavored, often with garlic, onion, and black pepper. The meat or fish is soaked in this preparation for as little as 30 minutes or as long as several days, depending on the recipe. Actually, marinades rarely penetrate a thick cut of meat very deeply, but they do add flavor to the finished dish.

Barbecue sauces also lend meat or fish a distinctive flavor, but since they are generally only brushed on the outside right before cooking, they do not penetrate very far, nor do they tenderize in any way. Most barbe-cue sauces contain oil which helps to keep the surface of the food moist during cooking; and they are often much thicker than marinades. Barbe-cue sauces are usually applied and reapplied frequently to the meat or fish during cooking. If the sauce is very thick this can create a wonderful crust on the outside of the food.

MARINADE TIPS

- An easy way to apply a marinade is to place the meat or fish in a plastic bag, pour in the marinade, and then tie the bag tightly. The bag can be turned occasionally to marinate the meat evenly.

- A marinade can be simmered to reduce it slightly and then used during the meal as a sauce, or as the base for another sauce.

BARBECUE SAUCE TIPS

- Most people like to use a brush to apply barbecue sauces. Some commercial brushes sold expressly for this purpose are very expensive. I suggest you start a collection of various sizes of paint brushes made of natural bristles. Wash the brushes with soap and water after each use and wrap them in waxed paper. Or, once they are dry, stand them, handle down, in an attractive wooden or earthenware cup near the barbecue.

- If you're ambitious enough to grill a whole pig, a haunch of beef, or large quantities of meat or fish, the barbecue sauce will be a lot easier to apply with a small cotton mop. There are small, short-handled mops available that are perfect for this purpose. It is impossible to be delicate when cooking in quantity on a grill, so don't worry if the sauce is not applied evenly.

- Barbecue sauces can be made ahead of time in a large quantity, and most of the following recipes can be doubled or tripled without much trouble, and refrigerated. Once you have found one you especially enjoy, make up a double recipe and keep it on hand for quick use whenever the mood to barbecue strikes.

❧ BRANDIED MARINADE

Use this as a well-flavored overnight marinade for chicken and pork. Tightly covered, it will keep in the refrigerator for up to one week.

> ½ cup brandy
> ¼ cup soy sauce
> 2 tablespoons unsulfured molasses
> ½ teaspoon Dijon mustard
> 1 tablespoon grated fresh ginger
> 1 clove garlic, minced
> ½ cup dry white wine

Blend together all the ingredients.
YIELD: ABOUT 1½ CUPS

❧ FRUITY MARINADE

The sweetness of this marinade makes it perfect for pork, but try it on beef as well. It is especially pleasant in the summertime. Coat the meat with it and let it sit in the refrigerator for several hours or overnight. Tightly covered, this marinade will keep in the refrigerator for several days.

> ½ cup pineapple juice
> ¼ cup orange juice
> 2 cloves garlic, minced
> 3 tablespoons dark brown sugar
> 2 tablespoons fresh lime juice
> 1 tablespoon turmeric
> ½ teaspoon ground coriander
> Salt and freshly ground black pepper to taste

Beat together all the ingredients.
YIELD: ABOUT ¾ CUP

❧ GAME MARINADE

The flavors of this marinade are hearty enough to stand up even to venison or wild goose. It is equally as good with lamb or less expensive cuts of beef. Pour it over meat and marinate at least 12 hours, turning the meat occasionally. Longer marination may be necessary for less expensive cuts of beef or older game. Tightly covered, this marinade will keep in the refrigerator for one week.

One 750-milliliter bottle full-bodied red wine
6 juniper berries, crushed
Pinch of Quatre Épices (a combination of spices, also sold as Beau Monde)
Pinch of ground nutmeg
1/4 cup olive oil
2 tablespoons red wine vinegar
1 bay leaf

Stir together all the ingredients.
YIELD: ABOUT 3 CUPS

❧ GARLIC AND HONEY MARINADE

Here is a sweet and sour mix for chicken, pork, and beef. Pour it over meat and marinate several hours or overnight, turning the meat occasionally. If desired, you can heat this marinade and brush it over meats while grilling. Tightly covered, it will keep in the refrigerator for up to one week.

1 small onion, minced
1/4 cup fresh lemon juice
1/4 cup sesame oil
2 tablespoons light soy sauce
2 cloves garlic, crushed
1 tablespoon grated fresh ginger
2 tablespoons honey
2 teaspoons chopped fresh parsley

Combine all the ingredients.
YIELD: ABOUT 1 CUP

❦ GARLIC AND ROSEMARY MARINADE

The combination of garlic and rosemary make this an ideal marinade for lamb. Try it with a butterflied leg of lamb for a special treat. Pour it over meat and marinate overnight. If desired, strain the marinade, boil it for 5 minutes and brush it over lamb while grilling. Tightly covered, it will keep in the refrigerator for up to one week.

>   1/2 cup dry red wine
>   2 tablespoons red wine vinegar
>   1/3 cup olive oil
>   4 cloves garlic, crushed
>   2 tablespoons fresh rosemary leaves
>   2 tablespoons chopped fresh parsley

Combine all the ingredients.
    YIELD: ABOUT 1 CUP

❦ GINGER GLAZE

Brushing this over roast pork, grilled ribs, or baked ham produces a wonderfully spicy sweet glaze. This mixture can be stored in the refrigerator for up to three days. Rewarm it over low heat before using.

>   1 tablespoon instant coffee
>   1/2 cup dry white wine
>   1/2 cup firmly packed dark brown sugar
>   1 teaspoon ground ginger
>   1/2 teaspoon Dijon mustard

Beat together all the ingredients. Simmer over low heat for 5 to 10 minutes. While the glaze is still warm, brush it over meat during the last 15 minutes of grilling to prevent the sugar in it from burning.
    YIELD: ABOUT 1 CUP

🦑 GARLIC SAUCE

The first time I was confronted with a variation of this sauce was in a Japanese restaurant where it was served with sautéed soft-shelled crabs. Never were they any better. Since then, this sauce has become a staple in my kitchen, where I use its flavors to complement almost any grilled or sautéed meat or fish. It is especially good with sautéed tuna steaks, pork chops, or roast lamb or when used as a basting sauce for grilled swordfish or salmon. It can be prepared up to two days in advance and stored in the refrigerator.

    1 tablespoon peanut oil
    4 cloves garlic, minced
    1 ½ tablespoons grated fresh ginger
    1 bunch scallions, white and light green parts only, chopped
    ½ cup dry white wine or rice wine
    2 tablespoons light or regular soy sauce
    2 tablespoons rice wine or dry sherry
    1 teaspoon sugar
    1 teaspoon white wine vinegar

Heat the oil in a large, heavy saucepan over medium heat. Add the garlic and ginger and sauté until transparent, about 3 minutes. Do not allow the mixture to burn. Stir in the scallions and sauté one minute more. Add the remaining ingredients and cook one minute longer. This sauce may be served hot or at room temperature.

YIELD: ABOUT 1 CUP

❧ HONEY MUSTARD MARINADE

Equally good for chicken, pork, or ribs, this tangy combination will quickly become a favorite. Marinate poultry or meat for several hours or overnight, turning occasionally. Tightly covered, this marinade will keep in the refrigerator for about one week.

> 1 cup Dijon mustard
> 1 cup dry white wine
> 3/4 cup olive oil
> 1/4 cup honey
> 1 clove garlic, minced
> 2 tablespoons soy sauce

Combine all the ingredients.

YIELD: ABOUT 2 1/2 CUPS

❧ HONEY SOY BASTING SAUCE

Similar to the preceding recipe, this sauce is meant to be used for basting meats during grilling. Use it for poultry, pork, or fish.

> 3 tablespoons Dijon mustard
> 3 tablespoons soy sauce
> 3 tablespoons honey
> 3 cloves garlic, minced
> 1/3 cup olive oil
> 3 tablespoons dry white wine

Combine all the ingredients in a small saucepan and boil over high heat for 2 minutes. Keep warm while basting.

YIELD: ABOUT 3/4 CUP

❦ LEMON BARBECUE SAUCE

This full-flavored combination gives citrus overtones to grilled beef, pork, poultry, and lamb. It is especially refreshing in hot weather. You can store this sauce in the refrigerator for up to two days, but remember to rewarm it over low heat before using.

2 tablespoons (¼ stick) butter
1 medium-size onion, finely chopped
2 cloves garlic, minced
¼ cup Easy Tomato Sauce (page 120)
¼ cup fresh lemon juice
1 tablespoon dark brown sugar
1 tablespoon Worcestershire sauce
1 tablespoon Dijon mustard
1 tablespoon grated lemon zest
Salt and freshly ground black pepper

Melt the butter in a small, heavy saucepan over medium heat. Add the onion and garlic and sauté just until transparent, about 5 to 8 minutes. Stir in the tomato sauce, lemon juice, brown sugar, Worcestershire sauce, mustard, zest, and seasonings, and simmer over low heat for 15 minutes. Apply the glaze while it's still warm.

YIELD: ABOUT ⅔ CUP

❦ LEMON MARINADE

Use this mixture for lamb or poultry. Try it with skewered shrimp for the grill.

2 tablespoons olive oil
½ small onion, finely minced
1 clove garlic, minced
2 tablespoons chopped fresh rosemary
Freshly ground black pepper
Grated zest of one lemon
¼ cup fresh lemon juice

Combine all the ingredients and use immediately.

YIELD: ABOUT ½ CUP

❧ LIME BASTING SAUCE

This tropical mixture is perfect for basting fish steaks or poultry while grilling. It will keep for a day or two in the refrigerator. Stir well and rewarm it over low heat before basting.

4 tablespoons (½ stick) butter
¼ cup fresh lime juice
2 tablespoons light soy sauce
3 scallions, both green and white parts, chopped
1 clove garlic, minced
½ cup dry white wine
1 teaspoon grated lime zest

Combine all the ingredients in a small saucepan and simmer over low heat for 10 to 15 minutes. Apply the sauce while it's still warm.

YIELD: ABOUT 1 CUP

❧ OLD-FASHIONED BARBECUE SAUCE

Why use commercial concoctions when this delicious mixture is so easy to make? Double the quantity and keep a jar in the refrigerator for up to two weeks for those spur-of-the-moment occasions when nothing will do but barbecue.

> 2 tablespoons olive oil
> 3 cloves garlic, minced
> 1 small onion, minced
> 2 cups catsup or tomato sauce (see Index)
> 1/2 cup unsulfured molasses
> 1/4 cup cider vinegar
> 1/4 cup Dijon mustard
> 1 tablespoon fresh lemon juice
> 1 teaspoon crushed red pepper
> Hot pepper sauce to taste

Heat the oil in a medium-size heavy saucepan over medium heat. Add the garlic and onion and sauté until transparent, about 5 to 8 minutes. Add the remaining ingredients and simmer over low heat for 20 minutes. Apply warm or cold.

YIELD: ABOUT 2½ CUPS

❧ PINEAPPLE MARINADE

You haven't tasted swordfish, dolphin, or mako shark until you have marinated them for several hours in this mixture. Try it on double thick pork chops, too. This is a wonderful marinade to keep on hand, and it can be stored for up to 5 days in the refrigerator.

> 1/3 cup pineapple juice
> 1/3 cup light soy sauce
> 1 tablespoon chopped fresh coriander (cilantro) or Italian (flatleaf) parsley
> 1/4 cup dry white wine
> Red (cayenne) pepper to taste

Thoroughly combine all the ingredients.

YIELD: ABOUT ¾ CUP

❧ ORIENTAL ORANGE MARINADE

The refreshing orange flavor of this marinade really brings out the best in a pork roast. Pour it over baby back ribs and marinate them overnight. Also try brushing it on ham steaks for a special treat. Tightly covered, this marinade will keep in the refrigerator for a week.

> ⅔ cup Seville (bitter) orange marmalade
> 1 cup orange juice
> ⅓ cup light soy sauce
> ⅓ cup catsup or tomato sauce (see Index)
> ¼ cup fresh lemon juice
> 2 cloves garlic, crushed
> 1 teaspoon grated fresh ginger
> ¼ cup peanut oil
> Freshly ground black pepper to taste

Beat together all the ingredients.
YIELD: ABOUT 2½ CUPS

❧ PLUM SAUCE

This fruity mixture can be used by itself as a sensational basting sauce for grilled ribs or roast pork, or add a few spoonfuls to enliven oriental dishes. It will keep for up to five days in the refrigerator.

> 4 large plums, pitted and chopped
> ½ cup vegetable oil
> ¼ cup light soy sauce
> ¼ cup orange juice
> ¼ cup dry white wine
> 1 tablespoon sugar
> 3 cloves garlic, minced
> Freshly ground black pepper to taste

Puree all the ingredients in a food processor or blender. Pour the mixture into a small, heavy saucepan and bring to a boil. Reduce the heat to low and simmer for 10 minutes. Keep the sauce warm if you're using it to baste.

YIELD: ABOUT 1½ CUPS

❧ PORK BARBECUE SAUCE

This combination has a definite Southern accent. The sweet overtones of this sauce provide the perfect foil for the richness of ribs and roasts in a way that no other sauce can. Try this: place a layer of rinsed sauerkraut in a roasting pan. Top it with ribs marinated in this sauce for several hours or overnight and roast them for about 1½ hours at 350°F, basting from time to time with the sauce. This wonderful sauce can be stored in the refrigerator for four or five days. Delicious!

> ½ cup firmly packed dark brown sugar
> ¼ cup unsulfured molasses
> 1 tablespoon dry mustard
> Salt and freshly ground black pepper to taste
> 1 cup dry white wine
> 1 cup cider vinegar
> ¼ cup fresh lemon juice
> 2 tablespoons hot pepper sauce
> ½ cup peanut oil
> ¼ pound (1 stick) butter

Bring all the ingredients to a boil in a small, heavy saucepan, mixing thoroughly. Reduce the heat to low and simmer for 10 to 15 minutes. Use this sauce while it's still warm.

YIELD: ABOUT 3½ CUPS

❧ RED CURRANT GLAZE

Europeans eat red and black currants with abandon. Yet their cultivation is rarely permitted in the United States because they harbor a fungus that causes the destruction of white pines. As a result, we have to satisfy our appetite for currants with commercial products such as jellies and preserves. This preparation uses red currant jelly and the result is a delicious, tartly sweet glaze for roast pork and ham. Brush it over the meat during the last 15 to 20 minutes of roasting or grilling. If you use it any earlier, the sugar in the jelly might burn.

> 1/2 cup red currant jelly
> 1 tablespoon fresh orange juice
> 1/2 cup dry white wine
> Freshly ground black pepper to taste

Combine all the ingredients in a small food processor or blender and process until smooth. Use immediately.

YIELD: ABOUT 1 CUP

❧ RED WINE MARINADE

This classic marinade can be used with almost any kind of meat or fish. Even chicken and veal chops will benefit from a few hours of soaking in this mixture of wine, oil, and seasonings. You can make this marinade up to five days in advance and store it in the refrigerator.

> 2 cups dry red wine
> 1 bunch scallions, both green and white parts, sliced
> 1 clove garlic, minced
> 1/2 cup olive oil
> 1/4 cup soy or teriyaki sauce
> 2 tablespoons dark brown sugar
> 1 teaspoon grated fresh ginger
> 1 tablespoon Worcestershire sauce

Combine all the ingredients. Use as is or boil it for 10 minutes over high heat and use as a basting sauce.

YIELD: ABOUT 3 CUPS

❦ RIB SAUCE

Pour this tangy sauce over ribs and refrigerate, covered, for at least several hours. Brush leftover sauce over the ribs while grilling or roasting. This mixture will keep in the refrigerator for up to five days.

> *3 tablespoons olive oil*
> *4 cloves garlic, minced*
> *⅓ cup firmly packed dark brown sugar*
> *¼ cup cider vinegar*
> *⅔ cup Chicken Stock (page 12)*
> *¼ cup tomato paste, sauce, (see Index) or catsup*
> *3 tablespoons Dijon mustard*
> *2 tablespoons soy sauce*
> *1 tablespoon crushed red pepper*

Heat the oil in a small, heavy saucepan over medium heat, add the garlic, and sauté until transparent, about 2 to 3 minutes. Do not allow it to burn. Beat in the remaining ingredients, reduce the heat to low, and simmer for 15 to 20 minutes until the mixture thickens.

YIELD: ABOUT 1½ CUPS

❦ ROSEMARY BASTING SAUCE

You can use this marinade and/or basting sauce for more than just lamb. A four-hour soak in this marinade will enhance pork, chicken, and venison roast, as well. If you want to make this marinade ahead of time, it will keep in the refrigerator for up to two days.

> *1 small onion, minced*
> *3 tablespoons Dijon mustard*
> *¼ cup light soy sauce*
> *1 tablespoon sugar*
> *2 tablespoons red wine vinegar*
> *2 tablespoons chopped fresh rosemary*
> *Freshly ground black pepper*
> *½ cup dry white wine*

Combine all the ingredients in a medium-size, heavy saucepan and simmer over low heat for 10 minutes. Use it for basting while warm.

YIELD: ABOUT 1 CUP

❦ SOY MARINADE

Marinate ribs, poultry, or duck for at least four hours in this dark, salty mixture and savor the oriental flavor of the finished dish.

> *1 cup soy sauce*
> *½ cup sugar*
> *1 bunch scallions, both green and white parts, chopped*
> *3 tablespoons sesame oil*
> *4 large cloves garlic, minced*
> *2 tablespoons grated fresh ginger*

In a small, heavy saucepan, bring all the ingredients to a boil. Reduce the heat to low and simmer for 2 minutes. Remove from the heat and cool completely. Use immediately.

YIELD: ABOUT 1¼ CUPS

❧ SWEET AND SOUR SAUCE

Here's a change-of-pace basting sauce that will bring a touch of the Far East to your weekend barbecue. Brush it over fish steaks, pork chops, or ribs while grilling, and watch them disappear from the table in a hurry. This sauce can be prepared the day before and stored, tightly covered, in the refrigerator.

½ cup Peach Chutney (page 224)
1 cup pineapple juice
3 tablespoons sugar
2 tablespoons grated fresh ginger
¼ cup cider vinegar
2 tablespoons fresh lemon juice
¼ cup soy sauce

Puree the chutney in a food processor or blender. Transfer it to a small bowl, add all the remaining ingredients, and stir until smooth.

YIELD: ABOUT 2 CUPS

❧ TERIYAKI GRILLING SAUCE

A slightly stronger variation on the recipe for teriyaki sauce, this sauce is meant to cling to the fish or poultry you are grilling. Brush chops, roasts, or fillets with it while cooking. This sauce can be made ahead and stored in the refrigerator for up to five days.

¼ cup homemade (page 116) or commercial Teriyaki Sauce
3 tablespoons dry vermouth or white wine
2 tablespoons sesame oil
1 clove garlic, chopped
1 tablespoon chopped fresh ginger

Combine all the ingredients. Brush over meat or fish while grilling.

YIELD: ABOUT ½ CUP

❧ TERIYAKI SAUCE

Make your own teriyaki sauce and leave the commercial variety on the grocer's shelf. Like many other things, this homemade mixture is far better than store-bought. Use it for marinating or basting pork, poultry, or fish. My children love it spooned over rice. This sauce can be refrigerated for up to two weeks.

½ cup Chicken Stock (page 12)
¼ cup dry vermouth
3 tablespoons light soy sauce
1 teaspoon sugar
2 tablespoons fresh lime juice
1 tablespoon minced fresh ginger

Thoroughly combine all the ingredients.
    YIELD: ABOUT 1 CUP

❧ THREE PEPPER MARINADE

While this spicy marinade is used essentially for pickling shrimp, it is also good for crayfish, lobster, or prawns. Pour the hot liquid over lightly cooked shrimp, allow the mixture to cool, and then chill several hours before serving. If desired, you can store this marinade in the refrigerator for up to three days.

1 cup white wine vinegar
1 small red onion, thinly sliced
1 teaspoon crushed red pepper
½ teaspoon whole black peppercorns
1 tablespoon whole green peppercorns
1 teaspoon whole pink peppercorns
1 teaspoon allspice berries
1 teaspoon juniper berries
3 cloves garlic, minced
2 tablespoons chopped fresh dill
¼ cup olive oil

Combine all the ingredients in a small, heavy saucepan. Boil for 10 minutes over high heat. Use while still hot.

YIELD: ABOUT 1 ¼ CUPS

❦ VEGETABLE MARINADE

Here's a tart combination that is perfect for marinating vegetables. While it's still hot, pour it over artichoke hearts, tiny pickling onions, mushrooms, cauliflower, or other vegetables. Then cover and let stand, refrigerated, at least overnight. This marinade will keep in the refrigerator for up to one week.

> ¼ cup dry white wine
> ¼ cup white wine vinegar
> Salt and freshly ground black pepper to taste
> 2 cloves garlic, crushed
> ¼ teaspoon dried basil
> ¼ teaspoon dried thyme
> ¼ teaspoon dried oregano
> ⅓ cup olive oil

Bring all the ingredients to a boil in a small, heavy saucepan and let boil over high heat for a minute or two.

YIELD: ABOUT ¾ CUP

❧ VEGETABLE MARINADE II

This is a more robust marinade for vegetables. Pour it over hot, lightly steamed vegetables and marinate for several hours to develop the flavors. The vegetables make a wonderful addition to any antipasto spread or cocktail buffet. This marinade will keep in the refrigerator for up to one week.

    1 cup olive oil
    1/3 cup red wine vinegar
    1 bunch scallions, both green and white parts, thinly sliced
    1/4 cup catsup or tomato sauce (see Index)
    2 tablespoons sugar
    1 clove garlic, crushed
    Salt to taste
    2 tablespoons chopped fresh basil
    1 tablespoon chopped fresh thyme

Thoroughly combine all the ingredients.
YIELD: ABOUT 1 1/2 CUPS

❧ WHITE WINE MARINADE

Use this light-colored marinade for delicate meats and fish. Shellfish is delicious when grilled and basted with this. The lime juice lends just the right touch of tropical flavor. This marinade is best when made fresh.

    1 cup dry white wine
    1/2 cup olive oil
    1/2 cup fresh lime juice
    2 tablespoons chopped fresh oregano
    Salt and freshly ground black pepper to taste

Whisk together all the ingredients. Let stand one hour before using.
YIELD: ABOUT 2 CUPS

CHAPTER NINE

❧ *Tomato Sauces*

WHAT DID COOKS DO BEFORE THE TOMATO WAS INTRODUCED TO THE EURO-pean kitchen? Native to Peru, it did not find its way to Europe until after the Spaniards had begun their conquest of Mexico in the sixteenth century. While it was probably the Moors who introduced the tomato to the Italians and French, it isn't really known whether it arrived via a circuitous route from Morocco, or whether the Spanish Moors disseminated it. The Italian word for tomato is *pomodoro,* which is probably derived from *pomi di mori* or apples of the Moors. While the French now call tomatoes *tomates,* the original name was *pommes d'amour,* also probably derived from apples of the Moors.

The French took to the tomato immediately, but the English were not so receptive. For a long time the tomato was used only as an ornamental plant because the English knew that it was related to belladonna and deadly nightshade, both poisonous. They've finally come around, however, and now it would be difficult to imagine a world without the tomato. What would Americans do without ketchup?

Tomatoes are relatively new to our diet, however, widely available only since the mid nineteenth century. While there is nothing like a homegrown tomato for taste, texture, and nutritive value, commercial tomatoes do have their place. They have been bred to have a very thick skin in order to resist bruising in transit, but they are quite good in some cooked sauces. For raw sauces, homegrown tomatoes are best, but in midwinter whole, canned tomatoes packed in juice can be substituted. The canned varieties are not only nutritionally sound, they are also usually of very good quality and, when faced with the pale pink balls of wood in the supermarket, they make a much more flavorful substitute.

TOMATO SAUCE TIPS

- Many recipes call for peeling and seeding tomatoes, which is very simple to do. Drop the tomatoes in a large pot of boiling water for 2 to 3 minutes, remove them with a slotted spoon and the skins will slip off easily. Cut the tomatoes in half across and squeeze the halves over a bag or plate, and the seeds will fall right out. Then proceed with the recipe.

- Most tomato sauces can be stored in the refrigerator for a day or two and freeze quite well. Make more than you can use in one dish, freeze the rest, and have an instant sauce on hand for hectic days or when there is unexpected company.

❧ EASY TOMATO SAUCE

This nearly all-purpose sauce freezes extremely well. Make it often and put some away for a busy night dinner. When tomatoes are overwhelming the garden, make it in quantity and freeze. Then take it out on a cold winter's night for a little taste of summer. Serve this sauce with grilled fish or grilled, roasted, or baked chicken, cornish hen, or even turkey. And, for pasta, it is terrific.

> 2 tablespoons (1/4 stick) butter or olive oil
> 1 large onion, thinly sliced
> 2 to 3 cloves garlic, minced
> One 16-ounce can peeled tomatoes or 6 large, ripe tomatoes, peeled, seeded, and chopped
> 1 tablespoon chopped fresh basil or 1/2 teaspoon dried
> 1 tablespoon chopped fresh thyme or 1/2 teaspoon dried
> Salt and freshly ground black pepper to taste

Heat the butter in a large, heavy skillet over medium heat. Add the onions and sauté until soft, about 2 to 3 minutes. Add the garlic and sauté another 2 minutes. Reduce the heat to low and stir in the tomatoes and herbs. Simmer for 5 minutes (10 minutes if using fresh tomatoes), breaking up the tomatoes with your spoon. Season well with salt and pepper. Serve very hot.

YIELD: ABOUT 2 CUPS

🦋 FRA DIAVOLO

Here is a sauce with an Italian accent and the full-flavored warmth of hot peppers. Traditionally, it is served with fresh lobster cut into it just before it is poured over linguine. But you will want to keep it on hand for serving with shrimp, clams, grilled fish, and, of course, pasta of all kinds. It can be made the day before and refrigerated.

1/3 cup olive oil
1/2 large green bell pepper, seeded and chopped
2 cloves garlic, minced
1/2 small onion, minced
2 tablespoons chopped fresh parsley
4 large, ripe tomatoes, peeled, seeded, and chopped
3 tablespoons tomato paste
1/4 teaspoon (or more) crushed red pepper
Salt to taste

Heat the oil in a large, heavy saucepan over medium heat. Add the pepper, garlic, and onion, and sauté until transparent, about 5 to 8 minutes. Lower heat, stir in the parsley, and simmer 1 minute. Add the remaining ingredients and simmer over very low heat for 45 minutes, stirring from time to time.

YIELD: ABOUT 2 CUPS

❧ FRESH TOMATO SAUCE

Here is an uncooked sauce that is delicious spooned over hot or cold fish, poached or grilled. Toss with hot pasta for an instant dish.

> *4 large ripe tomatoes, peeled, seeded, and diced*
> *1 bunch scallions, white part only, thinly sliced*
> *2 large cloves garlic, crushed*
> *1 tablespoon chopped fresh oregano*
> *1 tablespoon chopped fresh basil*
> *1 tablespoon chopped fresh thyme*
> *1 tablespoon chopped fresh savory*
> *1/4 teaspoon crushed red pepper*
> *1/4 cup fresh lime juice*
> *Salt and freshly ground black pepper to taste*

Stir together all the ingredients in a medium-size mixing bowl and let stand at room temperature at least 2 hours to develop the flavors.

YIELD: ABOUT 2 CUPS

❧ GRILL SAUCE

While this could be just a barbecue sauce, its pronounced tomato taste gives this sauce more versatility. Besides brushing on grilled meats and fish, toss it with hot pasta or spoon it over rice.

> *3 tablespoons olive oil*
> *2 cloves garlic, minced*
> *2 large onions, thinly sliced*
> *2 tablespoons red wine vinegar*
> *1/4 cup dry red wine*
> *3 medium-size, ripe tomatoes, peeled, seeded, and chopped*
> *Salt and freshly ground black pepper*

Heat the oil in a medium-size, heavy skillet over medium heat. Add the garlic and onions and sauté until transparent, 5 to 8 minutes. Stir in the vinegar, wine, and tomatoes. Cover and simmer over low heat for 25 minutes, stirring from time to time. Season well.

YIELD: ABOUT 1 CUP

❦ HOT TOMATO SAUCE

Another multipurpose sauce that goes well with beef, fish, and pasta, this
sauce can be made in advance and frozen or kept in the refrigerator,
covered. It transforms even microwaved fish fillets into a special occasion
dish.

3 tablespoons olive oil
3 cloves garlic, minced
1 tablespoon chopped fresh rosemary
¼ teaspoon crushed red pepper
3 pounds ripe tomatoes, peeled, seeded, and chopped
Salt and freshly ground black pepper to taste

Heat the oil in a large, heavy skillet over medium heat. Add the garlic,
rosemary, and red pepper, and sauté for several minutes. Then add the
tomatoes, raise the heat, and bring the mixture to a hard boil, stirring,
until it has been reduced to a thick sauce, about 10 minutes. Puree in a
food processor if a smooth sauce is desired. Season well with salt and
pepper. Serve at room temperature.

YIELD: ABOUT 2 CUPS

LEEK AND TOMATO SAUCE

Chicken, fish of all kinds, and pasta are all enhanced by this creamy tomato sauce. The special taste of the leeks takes it out of the realm of the ordinary.

2 tablespoons olive oil
3 medium-size leeks, white part only, washed thoroughly, drained, and thinly sliced
3 large, ripe tomatoes, peeled, seeded, and chopped
½ cup Brown Stock (page 11) or White or Veal Stock (page 13)
½ cup heavy cream
1 tablespoon chopped fresh thyme
1 tablespoon chopped fresh oregano
Salt and freshly ground black pepper to taste

Heat the oil in a large, heavy skillet over medium heat. Add the leeks and sauté until soft, about 10 to 12 minutes. Stir in the tomatoes and simmer over low heat until soft, about 10 minutes. Add the stock, cream, and herbs and continue to simmer until thick, stirring occasionally, about 20 minutes. Season well with salt and pepper. Serve very hot.

YIELD: ABOUT 2 CUPS

MARINARA SAUCE

This is perhaps the most classic of all tomato sauces and it is offered here in a quantity large enough to freeze for future use. Add this basic tomato sauce to other ingredients to make more complex dishes, such as chicken cacciatore. As is, serve it with shellfish, fish, veal or pasta.

¼ cup olive oil
4 medium-size onions, diced
4 to 5 cloves garlic, minced
10 large, ripe tomatoes, peeled, seeded, and chopped
1 cup chopped fresh basil
1 teaspoon sugar
Salt and freshly ground black pepper to taste

Heat the oil in a large, heavy skillet over medium heat. Add the onions and garlic and sauté until transparent, about 5 to 8 minutes. Add the tomatoes and simmer gently over low heat for at least one hour, stirring until the tomatoes are broken up and the sauce is fairly smooth. Add the basil and sugar and season very well with salt and pepper.

YIELD: ABOUT 4 CUPS

❦ MARINARA SAUCE II

Here is a slightly more complex version of the preceding recipe. This hearty preparation is perfect for pasta. You can store this sauce for one or two days in the refrigerator. It also freezes very well, and the recipe can easily be doubled or tripled.

3 tablespoons olive oil
1 large onion, chopped
2 cloves garlic, minced
1 large carrot, peeled and chopped
3 pounds ripe Italian plum tomatoes, peeled, seeded, and chopped
One 6-ounce can tomato paste
2 teaspoons chopped fresh oregano
2 teaspoons chopped fresh basil
¾ cup dry red wine
½ pound fresh mushrooms, sliced
Salt and freshly ground black pepper to taste

In a large, heavy skillet, heat the olive oil over medium heat and sauté the onion and garlic until just transparent, about 5 to 8 minutes. Stir in all the other ingredients except the mushrooms, and simmer over low heat for 30 minutes. Add the mushrooms, season with salt and pepper to taste, and simmer 5 minutes longer. Serve very hot.

YIELD: ABOUT 3 CUPS

❧ MIDDLE EASTERN EGGPLANT SAUCE

Use this delightful sauce in many ways; serve it hot over pasta or at room temperature over cold boiled potatoes, cold poached fish, or any vegetable-based salad.

> 3 tablespoons olive oil
> 1 small eggplant, peeled and chopped
> 3 large, ripe tomatoes, peeled, seeded, and chopped
> 1 medium-size onion, chopped
> 4 cloves garlic, minced
> Salt and freshly ground black pepper to taste
> 1/4 cup oil-cured olives, pitted and chopped
> 1 bunch fresh parsley, chopped

Heat the oil in a large, heavy skillet over medium heat. Add the eggplant, tomatoes, onions, and garlic, season, and sauté until soft, at least 15 minutes. Pour the contents of the skillet into the bowl of a food processor. Add the olives and process the mixture until smooth. Stir in the parsley now, if serving hot. Or, cool to room temperature and stir in the parsley right before serving.

YIELD: ABOUT 2 CUPS

❧ MOLE SAUCE

The origins of this sauce are unclear. The story goes that a group of nuns at a Mexican mission were surprised when their bishop made an unannounced visit. With no time to plan, they were left to scavenge whatever was at hand in order to make a meal. That is the reason there is a little bit of a lot of things in this sauce. However, the use of unsweetened chocolate in sauces actually dates back to the Aztecs. In those days, unsweetened chocolate sauces were considered so refined that only the emperor and his guests were permitted to eat them.

No matter how it came to be, mole sauce is unusual and delicious. Today there are many versions of this sauce, though traditionally, *mole* simply means a sauce containing hot chiles. Normally served with turkey, it also goes well with chicken and pork.

> 1 small onion, quartered
> 2 poblano chiles, stemmed, seeded, and chopped
> 4 large, ripe tomatoes, peeled, seeded, and cut up
> 3 cloves garlic
> 1/4 cup bread crumbs
> 1/4 cup roasted or raw peanuts, chopped
> 1/4 cup blanched almonds, chopped
> 1/4 teaspoon ground cinnamon
> 1/2 teaspoon coarsely ground black pepper
> Salt to taste
> 2 ounces unsweetened chocolate, chopped
> 1/4 cup olive oil
> 2 cups Chicken Stock (page 12)
> 1 tablespoon sesame seeds, toasted

In a food processor, finely chop the onions, chiles, tomatoes, garlic, bread crumbs, and nuts. Take care not to puree, so that the mixture retains some texture.

Pour the mixture into a small bowl. Beat in the seasonings and chocolate and set aside. In a medium-size, heavy saucepan, heat the olive oil over medium heat. Stir in the chile mixture and cook for several minutes, or until the mixture is thick and the chocolate has melted. Stir in the chicken stock and continue to simmer the sauce over medium heat until the mixture is the consistency of very heavy cream and is very hot, about 20 minutes. Stir in sesame seeds and serve immediately.

YIELD: ABOUT 3 CUPS

❧ PASTA PRONTO SAUCE

This sauce takes about 15 minutes from start to finish, just about the same amount of time it takes to bring a kettle of water to a boil and cook the pasta—any kind of pasta. This nearly uncooked sauce reflects all the freshness of its ingredients, so it's important to choose the finest you can find. Once you get in the habit of making this sauce, you will want to use it for grilled fish and poultry, too.

> 3 tablespoons olive oil
> 1/4 small onion, minced
> 1/2 large green bell pepper, chopped
> 2 cloves garlic, minced
> 3 large, ripe tomatoes, peeled, seeded, and chopped
> 2 tablespoons chopped fresh oregano
> Hot pepper sauce to taste

Heat the oil in a heavy skillet over medium heat. Add the onion, pepper, and garlic, and sauté about 3 minutes. Add the tomato and oregano and season well with the hot sauce. Raise the heat slightly and cook about 3 to 5 minutes. Serve very hot.

YIELD: ABOUT 1 CUP

❧ RICOTTA AND TOMATO SAUCE

This quick, easy, uncooked sauce will be a busy day favorite. Serve it over steaming hot pasta or cooked vegetables.

> 15 ounces ricotta cheese
> 1/2 cup Chicken Stock (page 12), boiling
> 2 tablespoons freshly grated Parmesan cheese
> 2 tablespoons chopped fresh basil
> 3 large, ripe tomatoes, peeled, seeded, and chopped
> Freshly ground black pepper to taste

In a blender or food processor, combine the ricotta cheese, stock, and Parmesan cheese, and process until smooth. Turn the mixture into a bowl and stir in the basil and tomatoes. Season well with pepper and pour over hot pasta.

YIELD: ABOUT 3 CUPS

❧ PUTTANESCA SAUCE

In Italian *puttanesca* means "harlot's" sauce, probably because it is quick and easy to fix, and thus, could be prepared between "appointments." In any event, make it often—the taste of anchovies and capers is inspiring, especially over grilled swordfish or any kind of pasta.

2 *tablespoons olive oil*
2 *cloves garlic, minced*
6 *to 8 anchovy fillets, chopped*
6 *large, ripe tomatoes, peeled, seeded, and chopped*
1/4 *cup black olives, pitted and sliced*
1 *teaspoon capers, drained and chopped*
2 *tablespoons chopped fresh basil*
Pinch of crushed red pepper
Salt and freshly ground black pepper to taste

Heat the oil in a large, heavy skillet over low heat. Add the garlic and sauté for two minutes. Stir in the anchovies and cook gently until they almost melt, about 5 minutes. Add the tomatoes and simmer 10 minutes. Stir in the remaining ingredients and simmer over low heat for 20 to 30 minutes longer, until thickened.

YIELD: ABOUT 3 CUPS

❧ RUSTIC TOMATO SAUCE

Make this quick tomato sauce often, especially in the summer when ripe tomatoes are so easy to obtain and so full of flavor. You will love it with many foods, including eggs, pasta, rice, even grilled fish. This is not a sophisticated sauce—it comes straight from the farmhouse kitchen.

> 1 tablespoon olive oil
> 1/2 cup chopped onion
> 1 clove garlic, minced
> 4 large, ripe tomatoes, unpeeled and cut into large chunks
> 1 sprig fresh thyme
> Salt and freshly ground black pepper to taste

Heat the oil in a large, heavy skillet over medium heat. Add the onion and garlic and sauté until transparent, about 5 to 8 minutes. Stir in the tomatoes and thyme, cover and simmer over low heat for 10 minutes, stirring from time to time to break up the tomatoes. Season well. Serve hot.

YIELD: ABOUT 1 1/2 CUPS

❧ SICILIAN SAUCE

This rustic sauce is robust enough for a blustery winter night main dish. Serve it over any kind of pasta, especially one with plenty of nooks and crannies to trap the sauce. You can also spoon it over double thick veal chops, or partner it with grilled pork chops.

> 2 tablespoons olive oil
> 6 cloves garlic, minced
> 1 small eggplant, unpeeled, chopped
> 4 large, ripe tomatoes, peeled, seeded, and chopped
> 1 cup tomato sauce (see Index) or Marinara Sauce (page 124 or 125)
> 1/2 cup Marsala wine
> 2 tablespoons chopped fresh oregano
> 1/2 cup chopped fresh parsley
> Salt and freshly ground black pepper to taste

Heat the oil in a large, heavy saucepan over medium heat. Add the garlic and eggplant and simmer, stirring, until soft, at least 30 minutes. Stir in the remaining ingredients, one at a time, and simmer over low heat until very thick, about 20 to 30 minutes longer.

YIELD: ABOUT 3 CUPS

❧ SMOKY TOMATO SAUCE

It is the slab bacon that gives this sauce both its name and its special character. It is a robust sauce that will clash with delicate flavors, so use it by itself with pasta, or spoon it over full-flavored fish such as fresh grilled tuna or red snapper.

1/4 pound slab bacon, diced
1 large onion, chopped
1 clove garlic, minced
4 pounds ripe tomatoes, peeled, seeded, and chopped
1/2 cup dry red wine
1/2 cup Chicken Stock (page 12)
2 tablespoons chopped fresh basil
2 tablespoons chopped fresh oregano
Salt and freshly ground black pepper

Sauté the bacon in a large, heavy skillet over medium heat until browned, but not crisp. Add the onion and sauté until it is soft, about 5 to 8 minutes. Stir in the garlic and sauté 1 minute more. Add the tomatoes, wine, stock, and herbs. Lower the heat and simmer for 40 minutes. Transfer the sauce to a food processor and puree. Season and serve hot.

YIELD: ABOUT 2 1/2 CUPS

❦ TOMATO BASIL SAUCE

Make this in the summer when tomatoes are ripe and sweet and the basil full of fragrant flavor. Serve it with pasta, fish, or chicken.

> ¹/₄ cup olive oil
> 3 large onions, sliced
> 4 cloves garlic, minced
> 5 pounds ripe tomatoes, peeled, seeded, and finely chopped
> ³/₄ cup chopped fresh basil
> Salt and freshly ground black pepper to taste

Heat the oil in a large, heavy saucepan over medium heat. Add the onions and garlic and sauté about 20 minutes, or until the onion is soft and golden. Stir in the tomatoes and basil, reduce the heat to low, and simmer, uncovered, for about one hour. Season with salt and pepper. Serve hot.

YIELD: ABOUT 3 CUPS

❦ TOMATO CAPER SAUCE

The tang of capers in a sauce just seems to make it perfect with seafood. Pair this sauce with any kind of sautéed or grilled fish or shellfish. It's rich, delicious, and easy to make.

> 2 tablespoons olive oil
> 1 large onion, thinly sliced
> 1 clove garlic, minced
> 2 large, ripe tomatoes, peeled, seeded and chopped
> ¹/₃ cup dry white wine
> 1 tablespoon Dijon mustard
> 1 tablespoon capers, drained and chopped
> Salt and freshly ground black pepper to taste

Heat the oil in a medium-size, heavy saucepan over medium heat. Add the onion and sauté until transparent, about 5 to 8 minutes. Stir in the garlic and tomatoes and cook 10 minutes more. Add the wine, mustard, and capers, season well with salt and pepper, and simmer over low heat until thickened, about 15 minutes. Serve hot.

YIELD: ABOUT 1 CUP

❧ TOMATO CREAM

The addition of a small amount of cream to this sauce makes it a smooth, elegant addition to shellfish, grilled fish, or even pasta for a colorful first course.

¼ pound (1 stick) butter, cut into tablespoons
3 large shallots, minced
2 medium-size, ripe tomatoes, peeled, seeded, and chopped
½ cup dry red wine
⅓ cup heavy cream
2 tablespoons chopped fresh basil

Melt 2 tablespoons of the butter in a large, heavy skillet over medium heat. Add the shallots and sauté until soft, about 5 to 6 minutes. Then stir in the tomatoes and wine. Raise the heat to high and cook the mixture until the sauce is reduced by about one half, about 5 to 8 minutes.

Add the cream and boil until the mixture is reduced by about one third, about 5 minutes. Puree the sauce in a food processor or blender and return to the skillet. Over low heat, add the remaining butter by tablespoons, shaking the pan and stirring, until all the butter has been incorporated. The butter should not melt, but should remain thick and creamy like that in an emulsified butter sauce. Stir in the basil and serve immediately.

YIELD: ABOUT 1 CUP

✨ TOMATO PUREE

Not only will this sauce go well with boiled meats, poached fish, chicken, or pasta, it can also be used whenever tomato puree is called for in other recipes. This sauce will keep several days, covered, in the refrigerator, or up to one month in the freezer.

3 tablespoons butter
1/2 medium-size onion, minced
4 large, ripe tomatoes, seeded and quartered
2 tablespoons fresh lemon juice
Salt and freshly ground black pepper to taste

Melt one tablespoon of the butter in a large, heavy skillet over medium heat. Add the onion and sauté for 5 minutes. Then stir in the tomatoes and simmer over low heat for 20 minutes. Puree the mixture in a food processor, then return the sauce to the pan and, over low heat, beat in the remaining butter and lemon juice. Season well with salt and pepper and serve hot.

YIELD: ABOUT 1 CUP

CHAPTER TEN

❧ *Pasta Sauces*

ONE OF THE MOST WONDERFUL THINGS ABOUT PASTA IS THAT ALMOST ANY-
thing can be used as a sauce or accompaniment. For example, many of
the savory compound butters (see recipes beginning on page 87) are
ideal as instant sauces for nearly any kind of pasta or noodle. In this
section, I have included not only some of the more classic Italian sauces,
but some more modern variations that will meet the tastes of today's
pasta cook—you. Whether classic or modern, all of these sauces taste best
when made fresh right before the meal. So, unless otherwise noted in the
recipe, it's best not to refrigerate or freeze any of the sauces in this
section.

In Italy, pasta is usually a first course rather than a full meal. Generally, much less sauce is used than in the United States, and the pasta is
followed by a piece of meat or fish, a vegetable, and sometimes a salad.
Even in the remotest Italian mountain village this will be the pattern. I
think this is because pasta takes the edge off an appetite and much less
of the expensive cut of meat or fish is needed to satisfy a diner.

What constitutes a pasta sauce is limited only by the imagination
and ingenuity of the cook. Here is where your own whim can take over
and you can exercise your inventiveness to the fullest extent. Anything
in the refrigerator can be made into a topping for spaghetti, linguine, or
any pasta shape. The one thing to remember is that the larger the pasta
shape (such as rigatoni, radiatore, penne, etc.), the more it requires a
sauce with some body or it will slip right off and remain on the bottom
of the plate. These pastas can carry chunky combinations of meats and
vegetables with ease. The long thin strands (such as capellini or spaghetti) are wonderful with more liquid sauces—even one composed simply of olive oil and garlic with a sprinkling of Parmesan cheese.

Simple lunches or suppers of a hearty pasta dish, a crisp salad, and

lots of the crustiest bread you can find are among the most satisfying
meals you can serve. Even spur-of-the-moment hungers can be fed
quickly with a sauce tossed together from whatever is at hand. I used to
have a baby-sitter for my children who often made an enormous pan of
spaghetti with a sauce that used a can of corned beef hash as its base.
Sound awful? It was wonderful—and it wasn't only the children who
enjoyed it.

Use the best pasta you can find, and experiment until you find a
brand that pleases you. Keep in mind that fresh and dried noodles are
not the same animal and you should not avoid high-quality dried pasta
in favor of mediocre fresh. Again, you will need to keep sampling until
you find the perfect fresh pasta. Of course, if you make your own you will
have the satisfaction of knowing you have created the meal from start to
finish.

❧ BASIL PASTA SAUCE

Basil has long been associated with the wonderful foods of Italy. It seems
to have an affinity with pasta as well as salads, fish dishes, and other
delicious preparations. This creamy sauce makes an excellent first course
sauce served over spaghetti, rotelli, or almost any shape pasta. It is also
delicious with freshly cooked fish of all kinds. Make it in the summertime
when basil is at its most fragrant.

> *4 tablespoons (½ stick) butter*
> *5 cloves garlic, minced*
> *1 cup heavy cream*
> *⅓ cup freshly grated Parmesan cheese*
> *⅓ cup chopped fresh basil*
> *Freshly ground black pepper to taste*

Melt the butter in a medium-size, heavy saucepan over low heat. Add the
garlic, raise the heat slightly, and sauté until soft, being careful not to let
the garlic burn, about 2 to 3 minutes. Lower the heat again and stir in
the cream and grated cheese. Simmer for 10 minutes until the sauce is
slightly thickened. Then stir in the basil and season with pepper. Continue cooking until heated through, about 1 minute. Serve very hot over
pasta with more freshly grated Parmesan cheese.

YIELD: ABOUT 1½ CUPS

🦐 BOLOGNESE SAUCE

Here is a classic recipe for meat sauce. Not only is it perfect with all shapes and types of pasta, it is also delicious with eggplant Parmesan, grilled steak, and many other Italian preparations. By the way, butter is used in this recipe instead of olive oil because this dish comes from Bologna, in the northern part of Italy where butter reigns supreme. This sauce will keep for up to two days in the refrigerator, and up to three months in the freezer.

3 tablespoons butter (or olive oil, if preferred) *Pancetta is best*
1 medium-size onion, chopped
1 stalk celery, chopped
1 large carrot, chopped
1 clove (or more) garlic, minced
3/4 pound stewing beef, chopped; *1/2 lb lean hamburger + 1/2 lb pork*
4 large, ripe tomatoes, peeled, seeded, and chopped
1 tablespoon chopped fresh thyme
1/2 cup dry red wine
2 cups Brown Stock (page 11)
Salt and freshly ground black pepper to taste

Melt the butter in a large, heavy skillet over medium heat. Stir in the onions and sauté until transparent, about 5 minutes, being careful not to let them burn. Add the celery, carrot, and garlic, and continue to sauté over medium heat for 5 minutes longer. Add the beef and cook until well browned. Stir in the tomato, thyme, wine, and stock, reduce the heat to low, and simmer about 1 hour. Season well with salt and pepper. Serve hot.

YIELD: ABOUT 3 CUPS

*Cook pancetta
add onion
+ carrot + cel*

❧ CARBONARA

This sauce became popular in Italy after World War II. There is a theory that it was the American GI's and their love of eggs and bacon who were the inspiration for it. In any event, it combines several ingredients that were in very short supply during the war years, and may have been simply a reaction to the deprivation of that time. Regardless of why it was developed, it is a rich, delicious sauce for spaghetti or capellini. Note that except for the bacon, the sauce is cooked by the heat of the hot pasta with which you are serving it.

¼ pound slab bacon, diced
3 large eggs, slightly beaten
2 tablespoons (¼ stick) butter, melted
1 tablespoon olive oil
1 cup freshly grated Parmesan cheese
½ cup heavy cream
Salt and freshly ground black pepper to taste

Sauté the bacon in a large, heavy skillet over medium heat until crisp. Set aside. Beat together the eggs, butter, oil, cheese, and cream in a large mixing bowl, season, and toss cooked, steaming hot pasta with the sauce until thoroughly hot, but not overcooked. Toss with the bacon and serve very hot.

YIELD: ABOUT 1 CUP

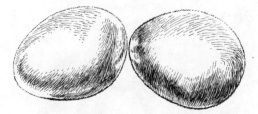

❧ CHICKEN LIVER AND TOMATO SAUCE

Here is a full-flavored sauce that will please anyone who loves chicken livers. Serve it with linguine or any pasta that needs a clinging sauce, such as rotelli, penne, fusilli, and so on.

> *¼ pound slab bacon, diced*
> *4 tablespoons (½ stick) butter*
> *1 large onion, chopped*
> *¾ cup (2 ounces) mushrooms, chopped*
> *½ pound chicken livers, trimmed and diced*
> *1 tablespoon flour*
> *2 tablespoons marsala*
> *1½ cups Chicken Stock (page 12)*
> *1 tablespoon tomato paste*
> *1 large, ripe tomato, peeled, seeded, and chopped*
> *Salt and freshly ground black pepper to taste*

Sauté the diced bacon in medium-size, heavy skillet over medium heat until crisp, then remove and let drain on paper towels till needed.

Melt 3 tablespoons of the butter in a large, heavy skillet over low to medium heat. Add the onion and sauté until transparent, about 5 minutes, being careful not to let it burn. Stir in the mushrooms and chicken livers. Sprinkle with the flour and stir. Stir in the marsala, stock, tomato paste, tomato, and bacon. Season with salt and pepper. Simmer over low heat for about 45 minutes, stirring from time to time. Swirl in the remaining tablespoon of butter and serve very hot over freshly cooked pasta.

YIELD: ABOUT 3 CUPS

❧ EGGPLANT SAUCE

This is an unusual, but classically Italian sauce. Not only is it delicious as a first course pasta sauce, but it complements roasted veal and poached eggs, as well.

> 2 tablespoons (¼ stick) butter
> 2 tablespoons olive oil
> 1 medium-size onion, chopped
> 1 medium-size eggplant, diced
> 2 large, ripe tomatoes, peeled, seeded, and chopped
> ¼ pound fresh mushrooms (wild, if possible, especially porcini), cut into large
>   pieces
> 1 teaspoon chopped fresh sage or oregano
> Salt and freshly ground black pepper to taste

Heat the butter and oil in a large, heavy skillet over medium heat. Add the onion and sauté until transparent, about 5 to 8 minutes; be careful not to let them burn. Stir in the eggplant, then add the tomatoes, mushrooms, and sage or oregano. Season well with salt and pepper and simmer, covered, over low heat for about 20 minutes. Serve very hot.

YIELD: ABOUT 2 CUPS

❧ GOAT CHEESE SAUCE

Serve this wonderful sauce over any flat pasta, such as linguine or fettuccine, or partner it with freshly steamed vegetables.

> ½ pound fresh goat cheese, cut into chunks
> 1 cup heavy cream
> ½ cup Chicken Stock (page 12)
> 2 cloves garlic, minced
> 3 tablespoons butter
> Salt and freshly ground white pepper to taste

In a heavy saucepan over low heat, combine the cheese, cream, stock, garlic, and butter. Stir until smooth, about 3 minutes, then season with salt and pepper. Serve very warm over freshly cooked pasta.

YIELD: ABOUT 2 CUPS

❧ FARMHOUSE SPAGHETTI SAUCE

In this age of pasta, variety is the spice of life. This delicious sauce which has its origins in the northern part of Italy is perfect for a simple supper. This recipe makes enough sauce for one pound of spaghetti or other pasta.

4 tablespoons (1/2 stick) butter or olive oil
1/4 pound mushrooms, coarsely chopped
1/2 pound prosciutto or other cooked ham, chopped
1/2 small onion, finely chopped
1 tablespoon tomato paste
1/4 cup water
1 pound fresh spinach or 1 box frozen spinach, completely defrosted, heated
        in a saucepan for 3 minutes over medium heat, drained, and finely
        chopped
1/4 pound fresh goat cheese, cut into chunks
Salt and freshly ground black pepper to taste

Heat the butter or olive oil in a large, heavy skillet over low heat. Add the mushrooms, prosciutto, and onion, increase the heat slightly, and sauté for 5 minutes. Stir in the tomato paste and water, reduce heat to low, and simmer for 20 minutes.

If using fresh spinach, wash it and shake off the excess water. Do not dry. Steam the spinach in a large saucepan over medium heat, using only the water clinging to its leaves, until just wilted, about 2 to 3 minutes. Drain and chop finely.

Stir together the hot spinach and goat cheese, until the cheese just melts. Season well with salt and pepper. Stir the spinach mixture into the mushroom mixture and cook over low heat for 1 minute. Toss with hot, cooked pasta and serve immediately.

YIELD: ABOUT 2 CUPS

❧ HAM AND WALNUT SAUCE

For those who like walnuts, this will become an instant favorite. Not only is it delicious with spaghetti or capellini, it is also an excellent accompaniment for grilled fish.

> 2 tablespoons (¼ stick) butter
> 1 tablespoon walnut oil
> 1 tablespoon chopped fresh basil
> 1½ cups (6 ounces) coarsely chopped walnuts
> ¼ pound boiled ham, diced
> ¾ cup heavy cream
> Salt and freshly ground black pepper to taste

Heat the butter and oil in a small, heavy saucepan over low heat. Add the basil, walnuts, and ham, then stir in the cream and simmer for 5 minutes. Season with salt and pepper. Serve hot.

YIELD: ABOUT 1½ CUPS

❧ HAZELNUT SAUCE

Here is another nut-based sauce, but it is entirely different in texture and flavor. Serve it over spaghetti or capellini, or any kind of homemade ravioli, especially one stuffed with goat cheese. It is also very good with cold pasta salads. This sauce can be prepared one or two days ahead and stored in the refrigerator. Do not freeze.

½ cup chopped hazelnuts
⅓ cup chopped fresh parsley
3 cloves garlic, minced
3 tablespoons fresh lemon juice
⅔ cup olive oil
3 tablespoons walnut oil
Salt and freshly ground pepper
3 tablespoons freshly grated Parmesan cheese

In a small mixing bowl, stir together the hazelnuts, parsley, and garlic, and then the lemon juice. Beat in the olive oil, a little at a time, until the sauce is thick, then beat in the walnut oil and season with salt, pepper, and cheese. Serve at room temperature over hot pasta.

YIELD: ABOUT 1½ CUPS

❧ MUSHROOM CHEESE SAUCE

This sauce is thick and creamy and goes very well with ravioli, fettuccine, and rotelli, as well as with roasted chicken. Serve it over freshly steamed vegetables, too. And for cheese lovers, it also makes a sensational substitute for macaroni and cheese!

> 1 tablespoon butter
> 2 large shallots, minced
> ½ cup chopped mushrooms
> 2 teaspoons hot curry powder
> 1 cup heavy cream, ¼ cup of it whipped to stiff peaks
> ½ cup Chicken Stock (page 12)
> ¼ cup fresh lemon juice
> Salt and freshly ground black pepper to taste
> ½ pound Gouda cheese, grated

Melt the butter in a large, heavy saucepan over medium heat. Add the shallots and sauté until transparent, about 3 to 5 minutes. Stir in the mushrooms and cook 1 minute more. Sprinkle the mushrooms with the curry powder and mix well. Stir in the unwhipped cream, stock, and lemon juice, season with salt and pepper, and continue to cook over medium heat another 10 minutes. Stir in the cheese. When melted, fold in the whipped cream and serve at once.

YIELD: ABOUT 2 CUPS

❧ PESTO

The subtle flavors of this basil-based sauce are superb when combined with a wide range of foods. While it is most commonly served with pasta, pesto can do wonders for broiled fish, sautéed veal, steamed vegetables, or even spread on slabs of freshly baked bread. Best of all, you can make it in large quantities and store it in the refrigerator (covered with ¼ inch of olive oil) for six months!

2 cups fresh basil leaves (the sauce will not work with dried basil)
¼ cup pine nuts
3 cloves garlic
½ cup freshly grated Parmesan cheese
½ cup olive oil
Salt and freshly ground black pepper to taste

Place all the ingredients in the workbowl of a food processor and process until smooth, stopping occasionally to scrape down the sides of the bowl. Toss with hot, cooked pasta and serve immediately or store refrigerated in a tightly sealed jar.

YIELD: ABOUT 1 ½ CUPS

❧ RED PEPPER SAUCE

This great sauce is not only invigorating to taste, it is delightful to the eye. The bright red of the peppers adds color to any plate of spaghetti. Serve it with spinach pasta for contrast, or spoon a little over roasted chicken or poached fish.

>   2 *tablespoons olive oil*
>   4 *large red bell peppers, roasted (page 155), peeled, seeded, and sliced*
>   1 *large onion, sliced*
>   1 or 2 *large cloves garlic, minced*
>   ½ *cup dry white wine*
>   ½ *cup heavy cream*
>   *Salt and freshly ground black pepper to taste*
>   2 *tablespoons chopped fresh parsley*

Heat the oil in a large, heavy skillet over medium heat. Add the peppers, onion, and garlic, and sauté until tender, about 5 minutes. Add the wine and simmer gently over low heat for about 20 minutes.

Remove the pot from the heat and transfer ⅔ of the mixture to the workbowl of a food processor and puree. Then return the puree to the skillet with the remaining ⅓ of the pepper mixture.

Stir in the cream, season well with salt and pepper, and simmer over very low heat for about 15 minutes. Stir in the parsley, simmer 5 minutes more, and serve very hot.

YIELD: ABOUT 2 CUPS

❦ SEAFOOD SAUCE

This delicious mixture of shellfish, wine, and mushrooms is at its best when served with capellini, the very thinnest pasta. Try it spooned over rice, as well, or atop tender fillets of sole or other small, delicate fish.

4 tablespoons (½ stick) butter
1 tablespoon flour
⅔ cup clam juice or Fish Stock (page 13)
¼ cup dry sherry
Salt and freshly ground black pepper to taste
1 large egg, beaten
2 tablespoons chopped fresh dill
½ cup (¼ pound) tiny shrimp, shelled
½ cup (¼ pound) crabmeat
¼ pound bay scallops
¼ pound button mushrooms, sautéed over medium heat in 1 tablespoon butter
*   until golden, about 5 minutes.*

Melt the butter in a large, heavy saucepan over medium heat. Stir in the flour and cook for one minute. Stir in the clam juice and sherry, stirring constantly until smooth. Season with salt and pepper.

Simmer the mixture over low heat until thick, about 5 minutes, stirring occasionally. Stir ¼ cup of the hot sauce into the beaten egg, then beat the egg mixture back into the rest of the sauce. Cook 1 minute, then stir in the dill, seafood, and mushrooms. Continue cooking over low heat until all the ingredients are heated through, but do not boil. Serve hot.

YIELD: ABOUT 2 CUPS

❧ SMOKED SALMON SAUCE

Pour this delightful sauce over fettuccine, or over very fine capellini for a more delicate dish. It is also wonderful with homemade ricotta-filled ravioli or spooned over plain omelets.

> 1 cup dry white wine, boiled over high heat until reduced by half
> 1 cup heavy cream
> 1 bunch scallions, white part only, thinly sliced
> 2 tablespoons salmon caviar
> 3 ounces smoked salmon, chopped
> Salt and freshly ground black pepper to taste
> 1 teaspoon chopped fresh dill

In a medium-size, heavy saucepan over high heat, boil the reduced wine, cream, and scallions until the liquid has been reduced by one third, about 6 to 8 minutes. Stir in the salmon caviar and salmon, season with salt and pepper, and stir in the dill. Serve over hot pasta.

YIELD: ABOUT 1 ½ CUPS

❧ SPINACH SAUCE

Serve this cream of spinach sauce when fresh spinach is at its peak. The delicate flavor is perfect with fresh pasta. Homemade ravioli will also benefit greatly from this colorful and delicious combination.

> 2 tablespoons (¼ stick) butter
> 1 large onion, minced
> 1 clove garlic, minced
> 1 cup heavy cream
> ½ cup Chicken Stock (page 12)
> 1 pound fresh spinach washed, steamed (using just the water clinging to the
>   leaves) for 3 minutes in a large saucepan over medium heat, then
>   drained, and pureed.
> Salt and freshly ground black pepper to taste

Heat the butter in a large, heavy saucepan over low heat. Add the onion and garlic and sauté until transparent, about 5 minutes. Add the cream and chicken stock and simmer gently for 2 minutes. Stir in the spinach and simmer 5 minutes longer. Season well with salt and pepper and serve hot over pasta.

YIELD: ABOUT 2 CUPS

❀ SPRING VEGETABLE SAUCE

This no-cook sauce is easy to make and absolutely delicious poured over hot pasta, mixed into pasta salads, served over grilled veal chops, or with cold poached fish.

> 2 large, ripe tomatoes, seeded and chopped
> 1 small zucchini, chopped
> 1/2 small cucumber, peeled, seeded, and chopped
> 1/2 large green bell pepper, seeded and chopped
> 1/2 large red bell pepper, seeded and chopped
> 1 bunch scallions (white and light green parts only), sliced
> 2 cloves garlic, minced
> 1 teaspoon chopped fresh thyme
> 3 tablespoons fresh lime juice
> 1/3 cup olive oil (or more if desired)
> Salt and freshly ground black pepper to taste

Toss all the ingredients together in a large mixing bowl. Chill overnight to allow the flavors to develop, but return to room temperature before serving.

YIELD: ABOUT 3 CUPS

❧ THREE CHEESE SAUCE

A simple but very rich sauce, this combination is best with spaghetti, capellini, linguine, or fettuccine. Serve it with crusty bread and a crisp green salad for a great winter lunch.

1 cup heavy cream
1/4 pound Gorgonzola or Roquefort cheese, crumbled
1/4 pound Comte or Swiss cheese, grated
1/2 pound Parmesan cheese, freshly grated
Salt and freshly ground white pepper to taste

Heat the cream in a large, heavy saucepan over low heat. When hot, stir in the cheeses in the order listed, waiting until each is thoroughly melted before adding the next. Stir constantly. Season well with salt and pepper. Pour over hot pasta and serve immediately.

YIELD: ABOUT 2 CUPS

❧ WALNUT GARLIC SAUCE

Another very nutty sauce, this one uncooked, that will be a favorite with homemade ravioli or any wide noodle. Try it with grilled fish, too, but make it a hearty one, like tuna. This sauce can be prepared one or two days in advance and stored in the refrigerator.

1/2 pound walnuts, chopped
10 cloves garlic
1 cup fresh bread crumbs, soaked in water to cover for 10 minutes and
  squeezed dry with hands
1/2 cup olive oil
1/4 cup white wine vinegar
Salt and freshly ground white pepper to taste

In the bowl of a food processor, combine the walnuts, garlic, and soaked crumbs. Pulse to mix. With the machine running, add the oil, vinegar, and seasonings through the feed tube and process until smooth. The sauce should be creamy. Add a little cold water if the sauce is too thick to pour. Serve at room temperature over hot pasta.

YIELD: ABOUT 3 CUPS

❦ WILD MUSHROOM SAUCE

For those who would die for anything made with fresh wild mushrooms, this sauce will become an instant favorite. It goes well with almost any pasta, and makes veal and chicken into something fit for a king or queen. You might even like to serve this sauce over toast, for a decadent late night supper or fantastic brunch. Choose any wild mushrooms that are available.

⅓ cup olive oil
3 cloves garlic, minced
1 tablespoon chopped fresh oregano
2 ounces dried porcini mushrooms (cepes), soaked in hot water for 10 minutes,
*   drained, dried with paper towels, and chopped*
2 ounces Shitake mushrooms, chopped
2 ounces brown domestic mushrooms, chopped
1 cup Brown Stock (page 11)
½ cup dry white wine
4 large, ripe tomatoes, peeled, seeded, and chopped
1 tablespoon chopped fresh thyme
Salt and freshly ground black pepper to taste
3 tablespoons chopped fresh parsley
½ cup heavy cream

Heat the oil in a large, heavy skillet over medium heat. Add the garlic, oregano, and mushrooms, and sauté for 2 minutes, tossing from time to time. Stir in the stock, wine, tomatoes, and thyme, and simmer over low heat for 15 minutes. Season well with salt and pepper, stir in parsley and cream, and simmer 10 minutes longer. Serve very hot.

YIELD: ABOUT 3 CUPS

❧ YOGURT AND PROSCIUTTO SAUCE

This is a lovely, quick supper dish for a busy day. Use the finest quality yogurt you can find.

> 2 tablespoons olive oil
> 1 bunch scallions (white and light green parts only) sliced
> 1/4 pound prosciutto, chopped
> 1 teaspoon chopped fresh marjoram
> 2 tablespoons chopped fresh parsley
> 1 1/2 cups plain yogurt
> Salt and freshly ground black pepper to taste

Heat the oil in a large, heavy skillet over low heat. Stir in the scallions and prosciutto and sauté for 5 minutes. Stir in herbs and yogurt and simmer for 5 minutes more. Season with salt and pepper and toss with hot, cooked pasta.

YIELD: ABOUT 1 1/2 CUPS

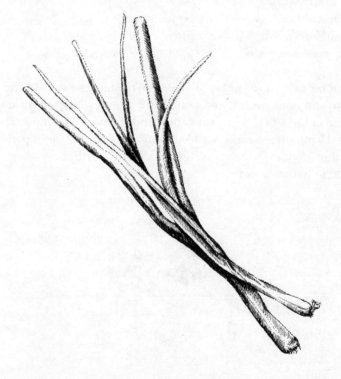

CHAPTER ELEVEN

❧ *Salsas*

SALSAS ARE UNCOMPLICATED COOKED OR UNCOOKED SAUCES THAT WILL RE-
quire some short preparation time, but will more than repay you with the
lively taste they add to any meal. Some of the sauces in this section are
based on the fresh and cooked salsas of Mexico and South America.
These fresh, often pepper-hot salsas are extraordinarily good with grilled
foods.

I find that several salsas set out on a summer table offer your guests
and family the opportunity to create their own special dish. Grilled fish,
shellfish, and meats, such as chicken, lamb, pork, or beef are wonderful
with a spoonful of these tangy mixtures as an accompaniment.

Best of all, many of them can be prepared ahead of time so that
putting dinner together is a quick and easy task. Cooked salsas can be
made up to 3 days in advance, while raw salsas should be made no earlier
than the day before.

SALSA TIPS

- Many of these salsas contain hot peppers, which, while wonderful to cook with, do require a few precautions. When
  preparing these peppers, it is often wise to wear rubber
  gloves, especially if you have sensitive skin. The enzyme
  capsaicin is ferociously irritating. Be very careful to wash
  your hands each time you handle the peppers, and DO NOT
  RUB YOUR EYES.

- Many salsas do not require the peppers to be skinned, only
  stemmed, halved, and seeded. If the skins are to be

removed, simply follow the directions for roasting and peeling peppers below.

• There are a dozen commonly available varieties of chiles.
The ones most widely used are Serrano, an exceptionally
hot, tiny little green pepper widely used in Mexico; jalapeño,
a jade green, slightly ovoid pepper that is extremely popular
in California and the Southwest, and that is almost as hot as
the Serrano; chipotle, a dried and smoked version of the
jalapeño that imparts a very distinctive flavor to certain
dishes that cannot be duplicated with anything else; Anaheim, a long, bright green, relatively mild pepper that is
usually peeled before incorporating into dishes such as
chiles rellenos (stuffed peppers); poblano, a large chile
often used in stuffings that can range from mild to hot and
is best when it's a blackish green; ancho, a dried poblano
that has fully ripened to red, has a full chile flavor; and dried
red peppers, which offer heat without preparation. But if
you crush them in your hands before adding them to a dish,
be sure to wash with soap and water before touching your
eyes.

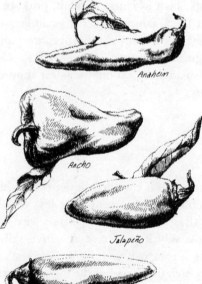

• Many of the recipes in this section and elsewhere in the book call for roasted peppers. All peppers, including chiles and bell peppers, can be roasted and peeled, in the following way:

Preheat the oven to 475°F. Place the whole peppers on a baking sheet and roast them turning occasionally until the skins blister all over, about 15 to 20 minutes. Place the hot peppers in a heavy paper or plastic bag, and seal tightly for about 10 minutes. Remove the peppers and the skins will rub or peel off easily. Peppers can be roasted on the grill before peeling, as well, a process that gives the final preparation a faint smoky taste. Simply turn the peppers on the grill until the skins are charred and blistered, about 20 to 30 minutes, and then seal in a plastic bag. Remove and peel.

❧ CHIPOTLE SAUCE

A chipotle pepper is a jalapeño pepper that has been dried and then smoked. It has a fascinating, very different smoky flavor that adds something special to this sauce. Serve this with chicken breasts, smoked turkey, or grilled fish. It keeps for about 10 days in the refrigerator.

½ cup dry white wine
4 dried chipotle peppers (available at gourmet food stores), stemmed and chopped
1 large red onion, chopped
2 medium-size, ripe tomatoes, peeled, seeded, and chopped

Simmer all the ingredients in a large, heavy saucepan over low heat for 30 minutes, then transfer the mixture to a food processor and puree. Chill for several hours to allow the flavors to develop, and return to room temperature before serving.

YIELD: ABOUT 1½ CUPS

❧ CRANBERRY SALSA

While cranberries do not grow South of the Border, this fresh relish does take on definite Mexican overtones with the addition of hot peppers and cilantro. Cranberries are a good source of vitamin C, especially when served raw. Why not add this to your traditional holiday menu, along with the more familiar cranberry preparations? You will be surprised how popular it will be. Roast pork will benefit from a little of this on the side, as well.

3 cups fresh or frozen cranberries, chopped
1 large onion, chopped
½ cup chopped fresh coriander (cilantro)
1 small hot red pepper
2 tablespoons grated orange zest
2 tablespoons fresh lemon juice
3 tablespoons honey
2 tablespoons orange juice

Combine all the ingredients in a large mixing bowl. Cover and refrigerate at least overnight in order to develop the flavors. Return to room temperature before serving.

YIELD: ABOUT 3½ CUPS

🦋 FRESH FRUIT SALSA

Grilled pork and pork roast never had it so good—and duck and game birds are not far behind. This sweet/tart sauce achieves just the right counterpoint of hot pepper and sweet fruit. Be sure to use the freshest of ingredients, expecially the coriander.

> 2 cups diced fresh pineapple
> 1 large red onion, diced
> 1 jalapeño pepper, seeded and chopped (be careful not to burn hands or eyes)
> 2 tablespoons red wine vinegar
> 3 tablespoons vegetable oil
> 1/2 cup chopped fresh coriander (cilantro)

Combine all the ingredients in a large mixing bowl and stir well. Cover and refrigerate 1 hour before serving to allow the flavors to develop. Return to room temperature before serving.

YIELD: ABOUT 2 1/2 CUPS

🦋 FRUITY SALSA

Almost like an uncooked chutney, this salsa improves with several hours of refrigeration. Like other salsas, it should be eaten at room temperature to take the most advantage of its complex combination of flavors. Serve it with grilled meats or fish.

> 1 green cooking apple, halved, cored, and minced
> 1 tablespoon fresh lime juice
> 1 small onion, minced
> 1/2 large red bell pepper, seeded and minced
> 2 tablespoons (or more) chopped fresh coriander (cilantro)
> 3 tablespoons olive oil
> Salt and freshly ground black pepper to taste
> 1 small jalapeño pepper, seeded and minced (be careful not to burn hands or eyes)

Stir together all the ingredients in a small mixing bowl, cover, and refrigerate for several hours or overnight. Serve at room temperature.

YIELD: ABOUT 1 1/2 CUPS

❧ FRESH VEGETABLE SALSA

As a condiment, sauce, or side dish, this fresh, uncooked salsa adds a
great deal to steamed shellfish or grilled fish. Partner it with cold roast
meats, too. The avocado is added at the last minute to prevent it from
softening and turning color. Do not peel or cut it up until just before
serving. Its creamy texture provides just the right contrast to the crunch
of the cucumbers and other fresh vegetables.

> 2 large, ripe tomatoes, cored, seeded, and finely chopped
> 1/2 small cucumber, seeded and chopped
> 1/2 small green bell pepper, seeded and chopped
> 2 scallions, both green and white parts, chopped
> 2 or 3 tablespoons chopped fresh coriander (cilantro)
> 2 cloves garlic, minced
> 1/4 cup fresh lime juice
> 1/2 cup tomato juice
> 3 tablespoons peanut or olive oil
> Salt and freshly ground black pepper to taste
> 1 large, ripe avocado

Combine all the ingredients thoroughly in a large mixing bowl except the
avocado. Season well with salt and pepper. Chill for several hours or
overnight. Just before serving, peel, stone, and chop the avocado and stir
it into the salsa. Serve at room temperature.

YIELD: ABOUT 3 CUPS

❦ GREEN SALSA

Made without tomatoes or red peppers, this uncooked salsa is indeed a lovely shade of green. It is, however, strong enough to take your breath away, so do not be fooled by its refreshing appearance. Served with grilled fish, beef, or pork, it can also liven up stews and sautéed shellfish.

> ½ cup fresh lime juice
> 1 bunch scallions, both green and white parts, chopped
> 2 jalapeño peppers, seeded and chopped (be careful not to burn hands or eyes)
> 1 cup chopped fresh coriander (cilantro)
> 3 tablespoons vegetable oil
> 1 clove garlic, minced

Combine all the ingredients in a large mixing bowl. Cover and refrigerate overnight or for several hours in order to develop the flavors. Serve at room temperature.

YIELD: ABOUT 2 CUPS

❦ OLIVE SALSA

While this uncooked salsa is delicious with grilled seafood and pork, it is a must on any summer buffet table. In fact, it's so good you might just want to put it on the table every night.

> 2 tablespoons olive oil
> 2 tablespoons red wine vinegar
> 2 tablespoons fresh lime juice
> 2 cloves garlic, chopped
> 1 bunch scallions (white and light green parts only), sliced
> 6 ounces oil-cured olives, pitted and chopped
> ½ to 1 whole jalapeño pepper, seeded and chopped (be careful not to burn hands or eyes)
> 1 tablespoon chopped fresh coriander (cilantro) or Italian flatleaf parsley

Combine all the ingredients in a small bowl, cover, and refrigerate overnight. Return to room temperature before serving.

YIELD: ABOUT 1 CUP

❦ PICO DE GALLO

Of all the uncooked salsas, this one is my favorite. It has a clean, fresh taste and can be made as hot as desired simply by adding more chile. Serve it with almost anything—fish, shellfish, pork, beef, or chicken. And it is the classic accompaniment to fajitas.

> *3 small, ripe tomatoes, cored, seeded, and chopped*
> *1/2 large red onion, chopped*
> *1 bunch scallions (white and light green parts only) chopped*
> *1/4 cup vegetable oil*
> *1/4 cup fresh lime juice*
> *1/4 cup chopped fresh coriander (cilantro)*
> *3 jalapeño peppers, seeded and chopped (be careful not to burn hands or eyes)*
> *Salt and freshly ground black pepper to taste*

Combine all the ingredients in a small bowl. Cover and chill overnight to allow flavors to develop. Return to room temperature before serving.

YIELD: ABOUT 1 1/4 CUPS

❦ PUMPKIN SALSA

Here is an unusual sauce that makes an interesting change of pace with grilled meats or fish. Try partnering it with curried chicken or lamb—it makes a terrific sideboy.

> *1 cup peeled and diced pumpkin, blanched in boiling water for 3 minutes, drained, and cooled*
> *2 large, ripe tomatoes, cored, seeded, and chopped*
> *2 jalapeño peppers, seeded and diced (be careful not to burn hands or eyes)*
> *1/2 medium-size red onion, diced*
> *1 clove garlic, minced*
> *1/4 cup chopped fresh coriander (cilantro)*
> *2 tablespoons olive oil*
> *Salt to taste*

Combine all the ingredients in a medium-size mixing bowl and let stand at room temperature for at least one hour, or refrigerate overnight to allow flavors to develop. Serve at room temperature.

YIELD: ABOUT 2 CUPS

❦ RAW SALSA

This simple raw relish has no hot pepper in it. For flavor it relies on the special marriage of lime juice, coriander, and garlic. Serve it with any grilled meat or fish, with salads, cold meats, and even with broiled veal chops. For something different on a hot summer day, toss this salsa with freshly cooked pasta.

> 2 large, ripe tomatoes, cored and chopped
> 1 large red onion, chopped
> 1/3 cup fresh lime juice
> 1 clove garlic, minced
> 1/3 cup olive oil
> 1/3 cup chopped fresh coriander (cilantro)
> Salt and freshly ground black pepper to taste

Combine all the ingredients in a medium-size mixing bowl and let stand several hours before serving at room temperature.

YIELD: ABOUT 2 CUPS

❦ RED SALSA

Made with tomatoes, red chiles, and red wine vinegar, this hearty salsa greatly enhances grilled vegetables, fish, and meats. Or partner it with a simple roast chicken and watch an ordinary dish take on a holiday taste!

> 2 large, ripe tomatoes, cored and chopped
> 2 ancho chiles, stemmed, seeded, and minced (be careful not to burn hands or eyes)
> 1 bunch scallions (white and light green parts only) chopped
> 2 tablespoons vegetable or olive oil
> 3 tablespoons red wine vinegar
> 1/4 cup chopped fresh coriander (cilantro)
> Salt and freshly ground black pepper to taste

Combine all the ingredients in a small mixing bowl. Cover and refrigerate several hours or overnight to allow the flavors to develop. Serve at room temperature.

YIELD: ABOUT 1 1/2 CUPS

❧ ROASTED RED PEPPER SALSA

The smoky taste of the roasted peppers, the saltiness of the olives, and the irreverent addition of Parmesan cheese add a very pleasing character to this very different sauce. It goes particularly well with charcoal-grilled swordfish, tuna, or shark.

2 large red bell peppers, roasted (page 155), peeled, seeded, & chopped
¹/₄ cup oil-cured olives, pitted and chopped
¹/₃ cup freshly grated Parmesan cheese
¹/₄ cup olive oil
2 tablespoons fresh lime juice
1 bunch scallions (white and light green parts only), chopped
3 tablespoons (or more) chopped fresh coriander (cilantro)
Salt and freshly ground black pepper to taste

Combine all the ingredients in a medium-size mixing bowl and refrigerate overnight. Allow the mixture to return to room temperature before serving. Stir well just before serving.

YIELD: ABOUT 2 CUPS

❧ TANGY LIME SALSA

Salsas can be used for everything from chip dips to steak sauces. You can vary the style by using either spicy jalapeño peppers or the milder canned green chiles. You can also top grilled fish, chicken, nachos, or even fresh salads with this mixture or use it on tacos and other traditional Mexican foods. Best of all, this salsa can be made ahead and stored in the refrigerator in a glass jar for one to two weeks.

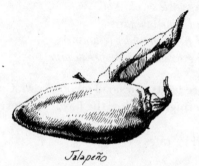

Jalapeño

2 large, ripe tomatoes, cored and chopped
1 medium-size onion, finely chopped
3 cloves garlic, minced
¼ cup fresh lime juice
1 jalapeño pepper, stemmed, seeded, and minced (be careful not to burn hands
    or eyes) or 2 canned whole green chiles
1 tablespoon dry white wine
1 teaspoon chili powder
Pinch of ground cumin
Pinch of sugar
Freshly ground black pepper to taste

Combine all the ingredients in a medium-size mixing bowl and let stand
at room temperature for one hour before serving.

YIELD: ABOUT 1½ CUPS

❧ TOMATILLO SALSA

Tomatillos are not relatives of the tomato, although in some parts of the
world they are called husk tomatoes. Their flavor is slightly acidic and in
Mexico they are often used in salsas and cooked sauces. This salsa goes
best with seafood, especially oysters, clams, and grilled or baked fish.

1 pound fresh tomatillos, hulled, stemmed, and chopped (or 2 small cans)
2 jalapeño peppers, stemmed, seeded, and minced (be careful not to burn hands
    or eyes)
1 bunch scallions (white and light green parts only), chopped
½ cup chopped fresh coriander (cilantro)
2 tablespoons fresh lime juice
Salt to taste

Combine all ingredients in a medium-size mixing bowl, cover, and refrigerate overnight to allow the flavors to develop. Serve at room temperature.

YIELD: ABOUT 1½ CUPS

CHAPTER TWELVE

❧ *Other Savory Sauces*

THIS SECTION CONTAINS AN ECLECTIC GROUP OF SAUCES THAT DON'T FIT INTO any fixed category. That does not mean that they are not wonderful combinations that you will want to serve often. They are.

Many of them contain yogurt and are lighter and less caloric than sauces elsewhere in this volume. Some, like the Herbed Avocado Sauce, are delicious with all kinds of meats and fish and could be used as a salad dressing as well. Others, like the Quick Horseradish Sauce, are so easy to make they can be whipped up at the very last minute to enhance a simple dinner of boiled beef or leftover roast lamb.

These sauces will act as a steppingstone for your own inventions. Create your own combinations, note them down, and then repeat them or modify them until you have something truly satisfying.

❧ ANCHOVY SAUCE

Anchovies do not seem to occupy any sort of middle ground on people's palates. Either you love them, or you can't stand them and pick them out of any dish in which they appear. For anchovy lovers, however, this sauce will be like manna from heaven. Serve it over poached or grilled fish, or, even better, with boiled potatoes. For a change of pace, use it to top open-face grilled cheese sandwiches made with mozzarella. This sauce can be prepared one or two days in advance and stored in the refrigerator. Stir well before serving.

3 ounces canned anchovy fillets, soaked in warm water for 20 minutes, rinsed
   well, and dried.
1 clove garlic, minced
1 tablespoon white wine vinegar
³/₄ cup olive oil
Salt and freshly ground black pepper to taste
1 tablespoon chopped fresh parsley

Mash the anchovies and garlic into a thick paste in a medium-size mixing
bowl and stir in the vinegar. Beat in the oil, a little at a time, until the
sauce thickens. Beat in any remaining oil in a steady stream. Season with
salt and pepper. Just before serving, stir in the parsley.

   YIELD: ABOUT 1 CUP

❧ AVOCADO SAUCE

Ripe, creamy avocados are perfect as sauce bases. This one has just a hint
of the flavor of guacamole in it, but it's thin enough to pour over grilled
fish or poultry.

2 large, ripe avocados, peeled, stoned, and chopped
1 small onion, quartered
¹/₃ cup milk
¹/₃ cup sour cream
Salt and freshly ground black pepper to taste
2 tablespoons chopped fresh coriander (cilantro)
Hot pepper sauce to taste

Combine the avocados and onions in the workbowl of a food processor
and puree. Transfer the mixture to a large mixing bowl and combine with
the milk and sour cream. Season well with salt and pepper, then add the
coriander and hot pepper sauce to taste. Refrigerate, covered, for several
hours or overnight. Return to room temperature before serving.

   YIELD: ABOUT 2 CUPS

❦ COLD CURRY SAUCE

Yogurt is a great sauce base. It has a low fat content, few calories, and a smooth, acid taste. Serve this curry sauce with cold roasted meats and fish, or use it to moisten vegetable salads.

1 cup plain yogurt
¼ cup heavy cream
1 tablespoon curry powder
½ teaspoon finely chopped fresh ginger
Salt and freshly ground black pepper to taste

Beat together all the ingredients thoroughly in a small bowl. Chill, covered, for several hours or overnight to develop the flavors and beat again before serving. Serve chilled.

YIELD: ABOUT 1½ CUPS

❦ COLD MUSTARD SAUCE

Mustard sauces are as varied as their uses. This one is elegant and deserves to appear on the fanciest tables. While it is not a quick sauce, you will find that the end result is truly worth the time and effort. Serve it with grilled meats, grilled vegetables, or cold poached fish.

4 large egg yolks
1 clove garlic, minced
⅓ cup Dijon mustard
¼ cup dry white wine
1 tablespoon water
2 tablespoons (¼ stick) butter, softened
½ cup heavy cream

In the top of a double boiler, over simmering water, beat together the egg yolks, garlic, mustard, wine, and water. Cook, beating constantly, until thick and frothy, about 10 minutes. Then beat in the butter. As soon as incorporated, remove the mixture from the heat and allow it to cool. Chill, covered, for 2 to 3 hours or overnight.

Whip the cream until stiff. Set aside. Beat the sauce until smooth, then fold the whipped cream into the mustard mixture and serve cold.

YIELD: ABOUT 2 CUPS

COLD YOGURT SAUCE

Yogurt has a fine, yeasty taste that goes very well with many kinds of fish. This chunky, salad-like combination should be on many summer menus—especially when grilled or poached fish is being served.

¾ cup plain yogurt
1 small cucumber, seeded and finely chopped
1 small, ripe tomato, peeled, seeded, and finely chopped
3 scallions (white and light green parts only), very finely sliced
1 teaspoon curry powder
1 teaspoon chopped fresh coriander (cilantro)
Salt and freshly ground black pepper to taste

Combine all the ingredients thoroughly in a small bowl. Chill, covered, overnight. Just before serving, check seasonings, adding more salt and pepper, if necessary. Serve chilled.

YIELD: ABOUT 1½ CUPS

✎ CUMBERLAND SAUCE

This sauce would be just as much at home on the dining table in a Jane Austen novel as it is in contemporary society. This sweet/sour preparation is still as good as it ever was with all types of cold roast meat, including poultry and lamb, but it really comes into its own with game. Venison, boar, and wild birds of many varieties are delicious with this old English sauce.

> *2 large shallots, minced, blanched in boiling water for 3 minutes, and drained.*
> *Zest of 1 orange and 1 lemon, minced, blanched in boiling water for 1 minute, and drained*
> *½ cup red currant jelly*
> *¼ cup ruby port*
> *¼ cup orange juice*
> *1 teaspoon cornstarch*
> *1 teaspoon dry mustard*
> *½ teaspoon ground ginger*
> *1 teaspoon fresh lemon juice*
> *2 tablespoons Grand Marnier or other orange liqueur*

Combine the shallots, zest, jelly, port, and orange juice in a medium-size, heavy saucepan and cook over low heat until the jelly has melted.

Meanwhile, combine the cornstarch, mustard, and ginger in a small bowl. Beat in the lemon juice and stir until smooth. Stir this mixture into the hot jelly. Bring the sauce to a boil, reduce the heat to low and simmer gently until the sauce is clear and thickened, about 5 to 7 minutes. Stir in the Grand Marnier, and serve hot or cold.

YIELD: ABOUT 1 CUP

❦ CURRIED YOGURT SAUCE

Yogurt is generally thought of as something that is eaten or served cold. This sauce proves that it can be equally delicious in a hot preparation. If you are lucky enough to have a spit roaster in your oven, roast a young chicken or two and serve them with this very tasty mixture.

> 2 tablespoons (¼ stick) butter
> 2 large onions, thinly sliced
> 1 tablespoon chopped fresh ginger
> 3 cloves garlic, minced
> 1 tablespoon curry powder
> 1 tablespoon flour
> 1 cup Chicken Stock (page 12)
> ½ cup pignoli nuts, ground
> 1 cup plain yogurt
> Salt and freshly ground black pepper to taste

Melt the butter in a large, heavy skillet over medium heat. Sauté the onions until transparent, about 5 minutes. Add the ginger, garlic, and curry powder, then stir in the flour and stock and cook one minute longer. Raise the heat to bring the mixture to a boil, then remove the pan from the heat and add the nuts and yogurt. Season well with salt and pepper. Serve immediately.

YIELD: ABOUT 3 CUPS

❧ FRESH VEGETABLE SAUCE

More like an uncooked relish than a real sauce, this tangy combination of summer vegetables and herbs is perfect for all your barbecue menus. Make it often and serve it with cold cuts, as well. This mixture keeps for two to three days covered in the refrigerator.

2 large onions, diced
1 pound ripe tomatoes, cored, seeded, and diced
1 medium-size cucumber, seeded and diced
1 large red bell pepper, stemmed, seeded, and diced
¼ cup diced cornichons or dill pickles
2 tablespoons capers, drained
1 tablespoon chopped fresh tarragon
3 tablespoons chopped fresh parsley
½ cup olive oil
2 tablespoons red wine vinegar
¼ cup Dijon mustard
Salt and freshly ground black pepper to taste

Combine all the ingredients thoroughly in a large mixing bowl and refrigerate at least overnight in order to fully develop the flavors. Stir again before serving. Serve chilled.

YIELD: ABOUT 3 CUPS

🕷 GAME SAUCE

While sweet sauces are traditionally served with game, this one is also perfect for dressing cold meats, especially pork. It will do double duty as well as a spectacular topping for ice cream, any sweet steamed pudding, or over homemade pound cake. It keeps well in the refrigerator and can be made a week in advance and simply reheated thoroughly just before serving.

> 4 tablespoons (½ stick) butter, softened
> ½ teaspoon ground nutmeg
> ½ cup firmly packed light brown sugar
> 1 teaspoon grated fresh ginger
> ¼ cup chopped pistachio nuts
> ¼ cup dark rum
> ¼ cup brandy

In a medium-size, heavy saucepan, melt the butter over medium heat. Stir in the nutmeg, ⅓ cup of the sugar, the ginger, and pistachios, and cook for one minute, stirring. Beat in the rum and then the brandy, a little at a time. Stir in the remaining sugar and simmer over very low heat just until it has melted. Serve hot.

YIELD: ABOUT 1 CUP

❧ GINGER SAUCE

The Oriental origins of this sauce make it the perfect addition to any stir-fry dish you might be making. Try it with vegetables, such as broccoli or asparagus, or serve it with any roast, fried, or grilled pork, or charcoal grilled fish. Shellfish benefit from a little of this sauce as well. Make plenty; it doesn't seem to last long.

> 1/4 *cup light soy sauce*
> 1/4 *cup rice or white wine vinegar*
> 3 *tablespoons grated fresh ginger*
> 2 *cloves garlic, minced*
> 1 *tablespoon sesame oil*
> 2 *tablespoons peanut oil*
> *Hot pepper sauce to taste or a pinch of Chinese chili paste (available in most supermarkets)*

Whisk all the ingredients together in a small bowl. Let the sauce stand several hours unrefrigerated in order to allow the flavors to develop.

YIELD: ABOUT 1/2 CUP

❧ GREEK TSATSIKI

In Greece this can be served either as a salad or a sauce. If you wish to serve it as a salad, simply slice the cucumber after seeding, instead of dicing it. Serve this sauce/salad with baked fish and enjoy the creamy contrast of flavors.

> 1 *cup plain yogurt, made with goat's milk, if available*
> 2 *tablespoons chopped fresh mint*
> 1/2 *teaspoon salt*
> 1/4 *teaspoon paprika*
> 1/2 *small cucumber, peeled, seeded, and diced*

Beat together the yogurt, mint, salt, and paprika in a small mixing bowl. Stir in the cucumber and chill for several hours. Season with more salt before serving, if desired. Serve at once, chilled.

YIELD: ABOUT 1 1/2 CUPS

🍃 GREEN ONION SAUCE

Whether you call them green onions or scallions, these milder relatives of the large white or yellow onions perk up both raw and cooked sauces. If you desire a very mild onion taste, use only the white part of this slender vegetable, otherwise, the entire vegetable should be used. Serve this sauce with poached or grilled fish, shrimp, even steamed oysters.

> 1 cup sour cream
> 1 tablespoon fresh lime juice
> 2 scallions, both green and white parts, finely chopped
> 1 teaspoon Dijon mustard
> 1 teaspoon grated fresh ginger
> 2 tablespoons chopped fresh parsley
> Salt and freshly ground black pepper to taste

Beat all the ingredients together thoroughly in a small bowl and chill, covered, overnight. Allow to warm to room temperature, then beat vigorously just before serving.

YIELD: ABOUT 1½ CUPS

🍃 GREEN YOGURT SAUCE

It is the iron-rich goodness of spinach that provides the color for this sauce. Serve it with roasted poultry of all kinds.

> ½ pound fresh spinach, washed, heated for 3 minutes in a saucepan over medium heat (the water left on the leaves is all that is needed), and still hot
> 1 clove garlic, crushed
> 1 teaspoon chopped fresh oregano or ¼ teaspoon dried
> ¾ cup plain yogurt
> 1 tablespoon fresh lemon juice
> ½ small onion, chopped

Puree all the ingredients in a food processor and serve immediately while warm.

YIELD: ABOUT 2 CUPS

❧ HERBED AVOCADO SAUCE

This colorful, very flavorful sauce is delicious with steamed fish and steamed or grilled summer vegetables. Use the best quality yogurt you can find.

> 2 tablespoons fresh lemon juice
> 2 large, ripe avocados, peeled, stoned, and pureed
> ⅔ cup dry white wine
> ½ cup clam juice
> 1 clove garlic, minced
> 1 bunch watercress, chopped
> 1 bunch parsley, chopped
> 2 tablespoons chopped fresh basil
> 2 tablespoons chopped fresh chervil
> 1 tablespoon chopped fresh tarragon
> 3 tablespoons plain yogurt
> Salt and freshly ground black pepper to taste
> Hot pepper sauce to taste

Beat the lemon juice into the avocado puree and set aside.

In a large, heavy saucepan over medium heat, bring the wine, clam juice, and garlic to a boil. Stir in the watercress, parsley, basil, chervil, and tarragon, raise the heat and boil hard for 3 to 4 minutes.

Remove the herb mixture from the heat and allow it to cool slightly. Then transfer the mixture to a food processor and puree. Combine both purees with the yogurt and season with salt, pepper, and hot pepper sauce to taste. Serve warm.

YIELD: ABOUT 2 CUPS

❧ MIGNONETTE SAUCE

In France, this sauce is usually, if not exclusively, served with huge plat-
ters of assorted *fruits de mer,* or shellfish. Raw oysters, clams, sea urchins,
and so on, are served on ice with a small bowl of this sauce for each diner
to dip them in. There is something about the combination of flavors that
accentuates the fresh, salty taste of the sea in the seafood. For a change
of pace, you might want to serve this with roasted lamb as well. Use
champagne vinegar in this recipe, if you have it, or rice wine vinegar to
add a delightful, slightly sweet taste.

> *1 cup white wine vinegar*
> *1 clove garlic, minced*
> *3 large shallots, minced*
> *½ teaspoon freshly ground black pepper*

Combine all ingredients in a small bowl and serve immediately at room
temperature.

YIELD: ABOUT 1¼ CUPS

❧ MINT SAUCE

Commercial mint sauce is readily available, but this is so easy to fix and
so much better, there is really no reason to buy it. This sauce stores well
in the refrigerator (it keeps indefinitely)—but it is so good, there will be
very little left. Serve with roast lamb, or use it as an ingredient in more
complex sauces, such as Mint Hollandaise on page 61. This sauce can be
prepared one week in advance and refrigerated.

> *¼ cup finely chopped fresh mint*
> *1 tablespoon confectioners' sugar*
> *Salt and freshly ground black pepper to taste*
> *½ cup white wine or champagne vinegar*
> *¼ cup water*

In a small, heavy saucepan bring all the ingredients to a boil over high
heat. Boil hard for 3 minutes. Cool completely for several hours and chill
until ready to serve.

YIELD: ABOUT ⅔ CUP

❧ MINTED YOGURT SAUCE

There is a Middle Eastern flavor to this delightful yogurt-based sauce. Partner it with grilled fish, steamed vegetables, or roasted lamb. Use only the finest quality yogurt you can find. You can prepare this sauce up to two days in advance. Store in refrigerator.

> *1 cup plain yogurt*
> *⅓ cup fresh lemon juice*
> *3 or 4 tablespoons chopped fresh mint*
> *Salt and freshly ground black pepper to taste*

Beat all the ingredients thoroughly in a small bowl and refrigerate, covered, for at least 2 hours to develop the flavors. Allow the sauce to come to room temperature and beat well once more before serving.

YIELD: ABOUT 1 ⅓ CUPS

❧ MUSTARD SAUCE

Here is a simple, smooth, hot mustard sauce. If more flavor is in order, stir in more mustard. Serve this with roast standing ribs of beef, grilled steaks, London broil—or with any kind of fish. This sauce can be prepared one or two days in advance and stored in the refrigerator.

> *2 tablespoons Dijon mustard (or more to taste)*
> *1 cup heavy cream*
> *1 teaspoon cornstarch*
> *2 tablespoons water*

Combine the mustard and cream in a small, heavy saucepan and bring to a boil over high heat. Mix the cornstarch with the water to make a smooth paste, and stir it into the sauce. Bring the sauce just to a boil, stirring, and serve immediately, very hot.

YIELD: ABOUT 1 CUP

❦ ONION PEPPER SAUCE

While this very tasty sauce is meant to be served with cold roasted or grilled meats, it is also delicious with fish, shellfish—especially oysters and shrimp—and freshly cooked pasta of all kinds. This sauce can be prepared one or two days in advance and stored in the refrigerator, but the onion taste will become stronger.

> 3 tablespoons olive oil
> 3 large onions, sliced
> 2 large red bell peppers, roasted (page 155), skinned, seeded, and pureed
> 2 tablespoons tomato paste
> 2 tablespoons chopped fresh basil
> Salt and freshly ground black pepper to taste

Heat the oil in a large, heavy skillet over medium heat. Add the onions and sauté until golden brown, about 20 minutes. Transfer the onions to a food processor and puree.

In a medium-size mixing bowl, stir together the onion puree, pepper puree, tomato paste, and basil. Season with salt and pepper. Serve at room temperature.

YIELD: ABOUT 1½ CUPS

❧ PEANUT SAUCE

Here is an unusual sauce made up of a combination of flavors that will
be both familiar and exotic. Don't be shy with the hot sauce; it will add
character. This sauce is tasty with grilled pork or chicken. It will keep for
one to two days in the refrigerator, but remember to rewarm it over low
heat before serving.

> 1/2 cup creamy peanut butter
> 1/2 cup canned coconut cream
> 2 tablespoons soy sauce
> Hot pepper sauce to taste

Combine all the ingredients together in a small, heavy saucepan and
bring to a boil over medium heat. Simmer for 5 minutes and serve hot.
    YIELD: ABOUT 1 CUP

❧ QUICK HORSERADISH SAUCE

Whenever the fresh bite of horseradish is called for, this very quick,
delightful sauce will fit the bill. Of course, it goes well with roast beef, but
try it with other grilled meats as well, or raw oysters.

> 3/4 cup sour cream
> 1 tablespoon milk
> 2 or 3 tablespoons prepared horseradish, drained
> Hot pepper sauce to taste
> Salt to taste

Combine together all the ingredients thoroughly in a small bowl. Serve
immediately at room temperature.
    YIELD: ABOUT 1 CUP

❧ SATE SAUCE

Small skewers of grilled meat served with a variety of sauces, many of which contain peanuts, are common all over the Far East. This peanut sauce is generally thought to have originated in Indonesia. Used as a basting sauce for roasted pork or chicken, it will create a meal that is very special indeed. It will keep for one to two days in the refrigerator, but remember to return it to room temperature before serving.

> 5 tablespoons chunky peanut butter
> 2 tablespoons dry white wine
> 1 tablespoon soy sauce
> 2 teaspoons grated fresh ginger
> 1 large clove garlic, minced
> 1 teaspoon white or rice wine vinegar
> 2 tablespoons peanut oil
> 1/4 teaspoon crushed red pepper (or more to taste)

Beat together all the ingredients. Use as a basting sauce or serve at room temperature as a condiment.

YIELD: ABOUT 2/3 CUP

✻ SESAME SAUCE

Sesame seeds are cultivated almost worldwide. In the Middle East they are made into oil, paste, and even sweets. In Asia and Africa they are a major source of cooking oil and provide a large amount of plant protein. The taste is pronounced, nutty, and even stronger when the seeds have been freshly toasted. Serve this delicious sauce with fish steaks, roasted or baked poultry, or with vegetables, such as broccoli, cauliflower, or green beans.

> 2 tablespoons sesame oil
> 3 large shallots, minced
> 1 tablespoon grated fresh ginger
> 2 cloves garlic, minced
> ½ cup white wine vinegar
> ½ cup dry white wine
> ½ cup Chicken Stock (page 12)
> 2 tablespoons heavy cream
> 1 teaspoon sesame seeds, toasted and crushed
> Soy sauce to taste

Heat the oil in a medium-size, heavy saucepan over low heat. Add the shallots, ginger, and garlic, and sauté until transparent, about 3 minutes. Stir in the vinegar, wine, and stock, raise the heat to high, and boil until the liquid has been reduced by half. Remove the mixture from the heat and stir in the cream, sesame seeds, and soy sauce to taste. Serve immediately.

YIELD: ABOUT 1 CUP

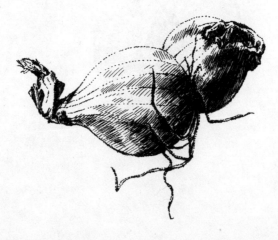

❧ SOUR CREAM SAUCE

Another delicious, fresh sauce that goes very well with poached fish. It can be prepared one day in advance.

> *1 cup sour cream*
> *1 tablespoon fresh lemon juice*
> *1 scallion (white and light green parts only), finely chopped*
> *2 tablespoons chopped fresh parsley*
> *1 tablespoon Dijon mustard*
> *1 tablespoon prepared horseradish*
> *1 teaspoon grated fresh ginger*
> *Salt and freshly ground black pepper to taste*

Combine all the ingredients thoroughly in a small bowl and chill, covered, for one hour to develop the flavors. Return to room temperature before serving.

YIELD: ABOUT 1 CUP

❧ SWEDISH MUSTARD SAUCE

This is a traditional sauce served with both gravlax and smoked salmon. Its particular flavor of sweet mustard and dill is a perfect partner to the rich, unctuous taste of salmon. You can make this sauce a day or two in advance and store it in the refrigerator.

> *¼ cup Dijon mustard*
> *2 large egg yolks*
> *1½ tablespoons sugar*
> *1½ tablespoons white wine vinegar*
> *3 tablespoons chopped fresh dill*
> *½ teaspoon dry mustard*

In a small bowl, whisk the Dijon mustard and yolks together. Beat in the sugar and vinegar, then stir in the dill and dry mustard. Refrigerate several hours to allow flavors to develop. Serve at room temperature.

YIELD: ABOUT ½ CUP

❧ SOUTH AMERICAN CHEESE SAUCE

The Monterey Jack cheese in this recipe takes the place of Mexican white cheese and it is a delicious substitute. Don't hesitate to serve this sauce with baked potatoes, broccoli, cauliflower, even omelets.

> ¼ cup olive oil
> 1 large onion, chopped
> 1 jalapeño pepper, seeded and minced (be careful not to burn hands or eyes)
> 2 large, ripe tomatoes, cored, seeded, and chopped
> ¼ cup chopped fresh coriander (cilantro)
> ⅓ cup dry white wine
> ⅔ cup heavy cream
> 1 cup shredded Monterey Jack cheese
> Salt and freshly ground black pepper to taste

Heat the oil in a large, heavy skillet over medium heat. Stir in the onion and pepper, and sauté until limp, about 5 minutes. Add the tomatoes and simmer over low heat for 15 minutes.

Stir in the coriander and wine and cook until thickened slightly, at least 10 minutes. Add the cream and cheese and simmer until melted, smooth, and very hot. Season with salt and pepper. Serve immediately.

YIELD: ABOUT 1½ CUPS

❧ SPICY MUSTARD SAUCE

This sauce gives you the opportunity to make your own mustard. It is time-consuming, but the quantity produced will last for several weeks in the refrigerator.

> 2 cups dry mustard
> 1 cup water
> 3 cups beer
> 2 cups cider vinegar
> 3 large onions, chopped
> 1 head garlic, peeled and minced
> 1 teaspoon dill seed
> 1 teaspoon dried tarragon
> 2 tablespoons grated fresh or prepared horseradish
> 1 teaspoon grated fresh ginger

In a medium-size mixing bowl, mix the mustard and water into a paste, then set aside. In a large, heavy saucepan, over medium heat, combine the beer, vinegar, onion, garlic, dill seed, and tarragon. Boil the mixture gently for 30 minutes, stirring from time to time.

Strain the liquid through a sieve and pour it into the top of a double boiler. Stir in the mustard paste and cook over boiling water until the mixture is reduced to two cups, about 1 hour, stirring from time to time. Stir in the horseradish and ginger, then remove the mustard from the heat and let it cool. Refrigerate, covered, for several days to develop the flavor. Serve at room temperature.

YIELD: ABOUT 2 CUPS

❧ SWEET RED PEPPER SAUCE

The distinctive flavor of sweet red peppers brings out the best in fish, chicken, grilled meats of all kinds, and grilled, boiled, or poached vegetables. This sauce can be made one day ahead and refrigerated.

> 3 tablespoons olive oil
> 3 large red bell peppers, stemmed, seeded, and chopped
> 2 large onions, chopped
> 2 cloves garlic, minced
> Salt and freshly ground black pepper to taste
> 2 tablespoons chopped fresh parsley

Heat the oil in a large, heavy skillet over medium heat. Add the peppers, onions, and garlic, and sauté until the onion is golden, stirring to prevent burning, about 15 minutes or longer. Transfer to a blender or food processor and puree. Stir in the seasonings and parsley. Serve warm.

YIELD: ABOUT 1 1/2 CUPS

❧ VEGETABLE MIGNONETTE SAUCE

This interesting variation of the classic French mignonette sauce is quite good with oysters and other *fruits de mer,* as well as roasted or grilled meats.

> 1 1/2 cups white wine vinegar
> 1 clove garlic, minced
> 2 large shallots, minced
> 3 tablespoons finely minced green bell pepper
> 1/2 large, ripe tomato, cored, seeded, and finely minced
> 1/2 teaspoon finely minced jalapeño pepper (be careful not to burn hands or eyes)
> 1/2 teaspoon freshly ground black pepper

Combine all the ingredients in a medium-size mixing bowl. Serve immediately at room temperature.

YIELD: ABOUT 2 CUPS

❧ YOGURT DILL SAUCE

This refreshing sauce brings out the best in lamb, as well as any kind of curry.

1 cup plain yogurt
1/2 medium-size cucumber, seeded and finely chopped
1 clove garlic, minced
2 tablespoons chopped fresh dill
Salt and freshly ground black pepper to taste
Hot pepper sauce to taste

Combine all the ingredients thoroughly in a small bowl. Chill, covered, for several hours before serving.

YIELD: ABOUT 1 1/2 CUPS

CHAPTER THIRTEEN

❦ *Salad Dressings*

NO MATTER WHAT IS BEING USED AS THE BASE FOR THE SALAD YOU ARE serving, it is the dressing that will make or break it.

Many composed salads that include meat or fish of some kind, vegetables, perhaps cheese, and, of course, greens, can be sauced with one of the mayonnaise recipes in this book (see Chapter 6). For tossed salads, however, the choices are almost endless and in this section there is a large selection for you to try.

Modern chefs often combine hot ingredients with cold. Usually these salads consist of a small amount of fresh greens, tossed with a savory dressing, and then topped with something hot, such as sweetbreads, a crisp soft-shelled crab, sautéed chicken livers, sautéed mushrooms, etc. These make very pretty, unusual, and not difficult first courses which will really please your family or guests. You could also try a slice of goat cheese which has been rolled in bread crumbs, sautéed in olive oil, and placed on top of the greens. This is a wonderful way to combine two classic French dinner courses—the salad and the cheese—either as a first course, or as a palate cleanser between the meat and the dessert.

SALAD DRESSING TIPS

● From the simple, very classic oil and vinegar which is tossed with a single kind of green and seasoned with salt and freshly ground pepper to a modern yogurt-based sauce, the key word is quality. Use the best ingredients you can find. Even the simple oil and vinegar is not without myriad variations: you can use olive oil (extra-virgin or virgin is best if you can find it), or walnut oil, sesame oil, or corn oil. Vinegars come in all flavors. Find combinations that you like and then keep on going.

- Except for those vegetable salads that are marinated, the dressing should only be applied at the last minute. Otherwise, the vinegar in many dressings will "cook," or wilt, the greens and the salad will become unappetizingly soggy.

- Most dressings are best if made just before serving. In France, for example, the dressing is usually made in the bottom of the bowl and the salad arranged on top; then the two are tossed together at the last minute. Unless otherwise indicated in the recipe, however, all the recipes in the section can be prepared a day or two in advance and refrigerated.

  Some salad dressings have a tendency to separate if prepared ahead, especially the classic vinaigrettes that are a combination of vinegar, mustard, oil, and flavorings. To prevent this, a tablespoon of cold water can be beaten into the vinegar and mustard before beating in the oil. Once the emulsification has taken place, it will usually hold up for several hours. Lately, I have seen cooks add an ice cube to the mustard and vinegar mixture which accomplishes the same thing. A little white wine added before the oil is beaten in will also help bind the dressing and adds a wonderfully different taste. However, if possible, do not chill your dressing. Fresh dressings have much more flavor than those that have been refrigerated.

- If the salad is to be served after the main course, I have seen talented chefs beat a tablespoon or two of the drippings from the meat into the dressing. This tends to carry the flavor of the main course into the salad and ties the whole meal together.

- A general ratio to follow when preparing any dressing is: 1 part vinegar or lemon (or lime) juice to 3 parts oil. If the oil has a very pronounced taste, such as walnut oil, you may want to use a combination of oils: 1 part flavored oil to 2 parts lighter salad oil. But remember that taste for salad dressings is very personal. Some people like them very tart and will therefore use more vinegar or lemon juice. Others prefer a more subtle flavor and will add more oil. In the end, it's up to you.

✤ BASIC VINAIGRETTE

Here is where it all starts. Before moving on to the other, more complex, recipes that are built upon this basic combination, it's a good idea to master the most simple of all. A teaspoon of water beaten into the mustard and vinegar helps hold the emulsion together and the result is a creamier dressing. Sometimes you can use wine or a little stock to provide a slightly heartier taste. Some people even beat the finished dressing with a little cracked ice. Don't laugh, it works.

> *1 tablespoon wine (white or red) vinegar*
> *½ teaspoon Dijon mustard*
> *1 teaspoon water*
> *Salt and freshly ground black pepper to taste*
> *¼ cup olive or other oil*

Whisk together the vinegar, mustard, water, salt, and pepper. Whisk in the oil in a steady stream. The mixture will thicken.

YIELD: ABOUT ½ CUP

BLUE CHEESE DRESSING

Blue cheese is a thrifty substitute for Roquefort or other expensive veined cheeses. The flavor is not as strong, but it will certainly make a delicious dressing.

> *1 cup Basic Mayonnaise (page 68)*
> *1/2 cup heavy cream*
> *2 tablespoons white wine vinegar*
> *2 ounces blue cheese, crumbled*
> *1 teaspoon brandy*

Stir together all the ingredients in a medium-size bowl. Chill several hours.

YIELD: ABOUT 2 CUPS

CAESAR DRESSING

While this dressing has definite Italian overtones, it was actually developed in California in the early 1920s. Traditionally served with torn leaves of romaine, it is delicious with any assortment of fresh greens.

> *1/2 cup olive oil*
> *1/2 teaspoon salt*
> *6 anchovy fillets, rinsed, dried, and cut up*
> *2 tablespoons fresh lemon juice*
> *1 large egg, coddled (soft-boiled) for 1 minute*
> *Freshly ground black pepper to taste*
> *1/2 cup freshly grated Parmesan cheese*

Put all the ingredients into a jar with a tightly fitting lid. Cover and shake well to mix thoroughly.

YIELD: ABOUT 1 CUP

❧ CAPER DRESSING

Pour this over cooled boiled potatoes and watch them disappear.

> 1/2 cup olive oil
> 1/4 cup white wine vinegar
> 2 tablespoons Dijon mustard
> 1 teaspoon dry white wine
> 1 tablespoon capers, drained
> Salt and freshly ground black pepper to taste

Put all the ingredients except for the salt and pepper in the workbowl of a small food processor or blender. Blend until smooth. Season well with salt and pepper, and use immediately.

YIELD: ABOUT 1 CUP

❧ CHEDDAR CHEESE DRESSING

Here is a cheddar cheese mixture that will really liven up vegetable salads. Serve it with any assortment of greens as well.

> 1 cup (4 ounces) grated cheddar cheese
> 1 1/2 ounces cream cheese
> 1/3 cup beer
> 1/2 cup heavy cream
> 1 clove garlic, crushed
> Pinch of crushed red pepper
> 2 tablespoons chopped fresh parsley

Beat together all the ingredients in a medium-size mixing bowl. Cover and let stand 1 hour before serving. Use immediately.

YIELD: ABOUT 2 CUPS

❧ CHUNKY PEPPER VINAIGRETTE

This might even be called Confetti Vinaigrette—it is colorful and fun to serve. With green beans it makes an instant vegetable salad. With slabs of iceberg lettuce, it makes eating greens exciting. With any assortment of greens, it is a perky, tasty dressing.

> 1/4 cup red wine vinegar
> 2 tablespoons Dijon mustard
> Salt and freshly ground black pepper to taste
> 2/3 cup olive oil
> 1/2 small onion, minced
> 1/3 cup minced green bell pepper
> 1/3 cup minced red bell pepper

Beat together the vinegar, mustard, salt, and pepper in a medium-size mixing bowl. Then whisk in the oil in a steady stream until thick. Stir in the onion and peppers. Chill for several hours. Return to room temperature and beat well just before serving.

YIELD: ABOUT 1 1/2 CUPS

❧ CLASSIC ROQUEFORT DRESSING

This is a more elegant version of the heavy concoction that is frequently served as Roquefort dressing. Serve this over mixed greens, or pass it with a salad of tomato and onions.

> 1 small clove garlic, minced
> 1 tablespoon Dijon mustard
> Salt to taste
> 1/4 cup white wine vinegar
> 3/4 cup olive oil
> 1/4 cup crumbled Roquefort cheese

Stir together the garlic, mustard, salt, and vinegar. Whisk in the olive oil in a steady stream until the mixture is thick. Stir in the cheese. Serve at room temperature.

YIELD: ABOUT 1 CUP

❦ CORIANDER VINAIGRETTE

The tangy flavor of this sauce enhances any salad, while remaining discreet. It is particularly impressive when served with cold poultry or cold poached fish.

> 2 tablespoons fresh lime juice
> ½ teaspoon salt
> Freshly ground black pepper to taste
> ½ small onion, minced
> 1 tablespoon minced red bell pepper
> 3 tablespoons chopped fresh coriander (cilantro)
> ⅓ cup olive oil

Beat together the lime juice, salt, black pepper, onion, bell pepper, and coriander, then whisk in the oil in a steady stream. Serve at room temperature.

YIELD: ABOUT ⅔ CUP

❦ CREAMY ITALIAN

Everyone seems to like this creamy dressing. Serve it with greens of any kind, or with fresh vegetables on a crudité platter.

> 1 cup Basic Mayonnaise (page 68)
> ¼ cup heavy cream
> 2 tablespoons white wine vinegar
> 1 clove garlic, minced
> 2 tablespoons chopped fresh oregano
> Salt and freshly ground black pepper to taste

Beat together all the ingredients and chill at least one hour. Return to room temperature before serving.

YIELD: ABOUT 1½ CUPS

❧ CREAMY JALAPEÑO DRESSING

Oh, the impact of these little peppers—they certainly add punch to any salad dressing. Be sure to wear rubber gloves when stripping the seeds and stem from the pepper, or do it under running water. Try this with fresh fruit salads for a truly different and delicious experience. Or serve it with mixed vegetables for a terrific side dish.

> ³/₄ cup plain yogurt
> 2 cloves garlic, minced
> 1 small jalapeño pepper, stemmed, seeded, and minced (be careful not to burn hands or eyes)
> 3 tablespoons chopped fresh coriander (cilantro)
> ½ teaspoon ground cumin
> Salt and freshly ground black pepper to taste

Combine all the ingredients in a small bowl and let stand for 2 hours before serving. Use at once.

YIELD: ABOUT 1 CUP

❧ CREAMY ORANGE DRESSING

Fresh fruit salads need a dressing with some character. The tang of yogurt and the spice of ginger make this a great combination with all kinds of fruit, especially citrus. Make this dressing no more than one day in advance.

> ¼ cup plain yogurt
> ¼ cup sour cream
> ¼ cup fresh orange juice
> 2 teaspoons fresh lemon juice
> 1 tablespoon honey
> 1 teaspoon grated fresh ginger
> 1 teaspoon grated orange zest

Beat together all the ingredients in a small bowl. Chill several hours and serve cold over fruit.

YIELD: ABOUT 1 CUP

❧ CREAMY ROQUEFORT DRESSING

This delicious example of the creamy Roquefort often served in steak houses and other restaurants can be made ahead and kept on hand for any occasion. Serve it with mixed vegetables, green salads of all kinds—or even as the binder for your favorite pasta combination.

½ cup sour cream
½ cup buttermilk
1 clove garlic, minced
1 tablespoon Dijon mustard
Freshly ground black pepper to taste
4 ounces Roquefort cheese, crumbled

Beat together the sour cream, buttermilk, garlic, mustard, and pepper in a medium-size mixing bowl. Stir in the cheese and chill several hours before serving.

YIELD: ABOUT 1½ CUPS

❧ DIJON YOGURT DRESSING

Yogurt and tofu make this a dressing that can be enjoyed even when dieting. Tofu can generally be found in the supermarket, or in Oriental grocery stores. This combination not only goes very well with greens, but can liven up plain poached fish or even cold roast pork.

6 ounces tofu (bean curd), squeezed and well drained
3 tablespoons fresh lemon juice
¾ cup plain yogurt
3 tablespoons chopped fresh parsley
¼ cup Dijon mustard
2 tablespoons snipped fresh chives (use scissors to snip)
Salt and freshly ground black pepper to taste

Puree the tofu with the lemon juice in a blender or food processor. Transfer the mixture to a medium-size mixing bowl, stir in the remaining ingredients, and chill several hours before serving. Serve chilled and use immediately.

YIELD: ABOUT 2 CUPS

❧ DILL AND BUTTERMILK DRESSING

The wonderful tang of buttermilk combines with the sweet fragrance of dill to make this dressing a refreshing summertime treat. Not only is it perfect for mixed salads, it is also delicious with crudités and other vegetable dishes. Better yet, use it to sauce your favorite pasta salad.

1/2 cup buttermilk
1/4 cup heavy cream
4 scallions, white part only, minced
1/3 cup chopped fresh dill
1 clove garlic, minced
2 tablespoons olive oil
1 tablespoon fresh lemon juice
Salt and freshly ground black pepper to taste

Put all the ingredients in the workbowl of a small food processor or blender and blend until smooth. Chill overnight to allow the flavors to develop fully. Return to room temperature before serving.

YIELD: ABOUT 1 CUP

❧ GINGER VINAIGRETTE

Use this dressing in any way you would use a classic vinaigrette—it goes especially well with warm potatoes and sausage.

1/3 cup olive oil
2 tablespoons white wine vinegar
1 tablespoon Dijon mustard
1 teaspoon soy sauce
1 clove garlic, minced
1 tablespoon chopped fresh ginger
Salt and freshly ground black pepper to taste

Whisk together all the ingredients. Serve at room temperature.

YIELD: ABOUT 1/2 CUP

❧ GREEK CHEESE DRESSING

Bring a taste of sunny Greece to the table when you sauce your salad with this feta-flavored dressing. Add a few oil-cured olives to complete the presentation. Make this no more than one day in advance.

> 2 ounces feta cheese, broken up into chunks
> 2 tablespoons dry red wine
> 3 tablespoons olive oil
> 1 clove garlic, minced
> 2 tablespoons chopped fresh oregano
> Salt and freshly ground black pepper to taste

Combine all the ingredients in a blender and blend until smooth. Chill at least one hour before serving. Serve chilled.

YIELD: ABOUT ½ CUP

❧ GREEN VINAIGRETTE

Here is an egg-thickened vinaigrette filled with the fragrant flavors of fresh herbs. Serve it with shellfish salads, sliced ripe tomatoes—or better yet, with homemade headcheese.

> 3 tablespoons red wine vinegar
> 1 tablespoon Dijon mustard
> 1 large egg yolk
> Salt and freshly ground black pepper to taste
> ⅔ cup olive oil
> 2 large shallots, minced
> 2 tablespoons snipped fresh chives (use scissors to snip)
> 2 tablespoons capers, drained
> ¼ cup chopped fresh parsley

Whisk together the vinegar, mustard, and egg yolk in a medium-size mixing bowl. Season with salt and pepper. Whisk in the olive oil in a steady stream until the dressing is thick. Stir in the shallots, chives, capers, and parsley. Let the dressing stand for about 30 minutes to develop the flavors. Beat once just before serving.

YIELD: ABOUT 1 CUP

❦ GUACAMOLE SAUCE

Ripe avocados are so easy to work with. Their creamy texture makes them the perfect base for salad dressings and other types of sauce. This thick mixture is great with sliced tomatoes and other vegetable salads, and goes wonderfully well with cold meats and broiled fish.

> 1 hard-boiled egg, peeled
> 2 teaspoons Dijon mustard
> 1/2 cup olive oil
> 2 large, ripe avocados, peeled, halved, and stoned
> 2 tablespoons fresh lemon juice
> 2 tablespoons chopped fresh parsley
> Salt and freshly ground black pepper to taste
> Heavy cream (optional)

In a large glass or porcelain bowl, mash the hardboiled egg with a fork until smooth, then beat in the mustard. Using a fork, beat in the olive oil, a little at a time, until the mixture is thick, like a mayonnaise.

In the workbowl of a food processor, process the avocados and lemon juice until smooth. Beat the avocado puree into the egg mixture. Stir in the parsley and season well with salt and pepper.

If a thinner sauce is desired, add heavy cream, one tablespoon at a time until the desired thickness has been obtained. Use at once. Serve at room temperature.

YIELD: ABOUT 2 CUPS

❧ HAZELNUT DRESSING

The nutty flavor of this dressing is excellent with fresh goat cheese—warmed or not—on a bed of mixed greens.

> ¼ cup white wine vinegar
> 1 large clove garlic, minced
> ¼ cup hazelnut oil
> ½ cup vegetable oil
> ½ cup hazelnuts, toasted
> Salt and freshly ground black pepper to taste

Put the vinegar and garlic in the workbowl of a small food processor or blender and blend until smooth. Whisk the oils together, then, with the machine running, add them in a thin stream. When the sauce thickens, add the nuts and mix until they are well chopped, but do not puree. Season with salt and pepper. Serve at room temperature.

YIELD: ABOUT 1¼ CUPS

❧ HORSERADISH DRESSING

Anyone who likes their Bloody Marys tangy with lots of horseradish, or who doctors up the seafood sauce until it is full of fire, will enjoy this two-alarmer. Serve it with a mixed green salad and watch the smoke detectors go off.

> ⅓ cup red wine vinegar
> ¼ cup sugar
> ¼ cup soy sauce
> 1 tablespoon grated fresh horseradish
> ½ cup olive oil
> Hot pepper sauce to taste

Stir together the vinegar, sugar, soy sauce, and horseradish in a small bowl. Whisk in the olive oil in a steady stream. Season with hot sauce.

YIELD: ABOUT 1 CUP

🦂 HOT BACON DRESSING

In the Deep South, this dressing is traditionally served with fresh field greens such as dandelion greens or chicory. The hot bacon and vinegar tend to wilt the somewhat tough leaves and dense stalks. Unless you grow your own "sallit," we suggest sampling this with fresh spinach, well washed, stemmed, and torn into bite-size pieces. Add a few garlicky croutons if you like. Or, use it to accompany grilled pork chops or roasted fresh ham. The slightly tart flavor will cut the richness of the meat.

> *2 ounces slab bacon, diced*
> *1 tablespoon flour*
> *2 tablespoons sugar*
> *1 large egg, beaten*
> *¼ cup cider vinegar*
> *1 cup water*
> *Salt and freshly ground black pepper to taste*

Fry the bacon until crisp. Remove it from the pan with a slotted spoon, leaving the drippings behind. Set pan aside. In a separate bowl, beat together the flour, sugar, egg, vinegar, and water. Stir the egg mixture into the hot bacon drippings and cook over low heat, stirring, until thick, about 3 to 5 minutes. Season well with salt and pepper. Pour over salad and toss. Serve at once.

YIELD: ABOUT 1 CUP

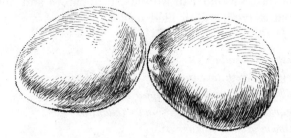

❧ JALAPEÑO VINAIGRETTE

The bite from this peppery vinaigrette brings a little South-of-the-Border taste to cold meat and shellfish salads.

⅔ cup olive oil
¼ cup red wine vinegar
1 tablespoon Dijon mustard
1 clove garlic, minced
½ teaspoon finely minced jalapeño pepper (be careful not to burn hands or eyes)
¼ cup chopped fresh coriander (cilantro)
Salt to taste

Whisk together all the ingredients in a medium-size mixing bowl. Let stand about 30 minutes before using to blend the flavors.

YIELD: ABOUT 1½ CUPS

❧ MARGARITA DRESSING

Tequila and lime juice—and a little salt—are the makings of a really potent Mexican cocktail. Here it is translated into a sensational salad dressing that tastes wonderful with sliced tomatoes and onions. For a fabulous treat, serve it with grilled scallops.

3 tablespoons tequila
3 tablespoons fresh lime juice
Salt and freshly ground black pepper to taste
2 tablespoons chopped fresh coriander (cilantro)
¼ teaspoon ground cumin
½ cup olive oil

Combine all the ingredients except the olive oil in a medium-size mixing bowl. Whisk in the oil a little at a time until the dressing becomes thick, then beat in the remaining oil in a steady stream.

YIELD: ABOUT ¾ CUP

✵ OLD-FASHIONED FRENCH DRESSING

When mother made salad dressing at home, this was it. Served with freshly boiled artichokes, green salads, citrus salads, or even cold meats, this is really an all-purpose dressing with lots of flavor. Mother used to put everything in a Mason jar and shake it all together to mix it. Try it, it works.

½ cup vegetable oil
¼ cup red wine vinegar
¼ cup good quality chili sauce
2 tablespoons sugar
1 teaspoon Dijon mustard
1 teaspoon Worcestershire sauce
½ small onion, minced
¼ teaspoon paprika
Salt to taste

Combine all the ingredients in a medium-size mixing bowl and beat well to blend. Let the dressing stand for at least an hour to blend the flavors.

YIELD: ABOUT 1½ CUPS

✵ ONION VINAIGRETTE

Vinaigrettes come in all flavors. This one is enhanced by the decidedly prominent taste of onion. Serve it with cold meat salads or with mixed salads of greens, tomatoes, and vegetables.

1 small onion, grated
2 tablespoons red wine vinegar
1 teaspoon chopped fresh dill
Salt and freshly ground black pepper to taste
½ cup olive oil

Whisk together all the ingredients until smooth in a medium-size mixing bowl.

YIELD: ABOUT ¾ CUP

❧ ORANGE YOGURT DRESSING

This is a decidedly orange dressing, with an entirely different flavor from the Creamy Orange Dressing on page 193. It is meant expressly for citrus salads—add a little sliced onion if you like—but also can be paired with any mixed fruit salad. In fact, it's almost sweet enough to serve over fruit for dessert. Make this dressing the same day you plan to use it.

> 1 tablespoon grated orange zest, blanched in boiling water for 1 minute, drained, and dried
> 2/3 cup fresh orange juice
> 1 teaspoon grated fresh ginger
> 2 tablespoons sugar
> 3/4 cup plain yogurt

Beat together all the ingredients in a medium-size mixing bowl. Chill for several hours before using.

YIELD: ABOUT 1½ CUPS

❧ ORIENTAL DRESSING

While this is definitely a salad dressing, it is also very good with roast pork, hot or cold. The hot, nutty flavor with just a touch of acid will also perk up any pasta salad and make grilled fish something extra special.

> 1 tablespoon lemon rind
> 1 clove garlic
> ½ cup peanut oil
> ¼ cup fresh lemon juice
> 1 tablespoon soy sauce
> 1 tablespoon rice or white wine vinegar
> 1 tablespoon peanut butter, chunky or smooth
> ½ teaspoon Chinese chili paste (available in most supermarkets)
> Salt to taste

Place the lemon rind and garlic in the workbowl of a food processor and pulse until finely chopped. Add the oil, lemon juice, soy sauce, vinegar, peanut butter, and chili paste, and process until the mixture is thick and creamy. Season with salt and serve at room temperature.

YIELD: ABOUT 1 CUP

❦ POPPYSEED DRESSING I

Here are three distinctly different poppyseed combinations. Serve this first one on citrus salads, with a few additional poppyseeds sprinkled on the top.

1/3 cup sugar
3 tablespoons cider vinegar
1 tablespoon grated onion
1 teaspoon dry mustard
1/2 teaspoon salt
2/3 cup vegetable oil
1 tablespoon poppyseeds

In a blender combine the sugar, vinegar, onion, mustard, and salt, and blend until smooth. With the blender running, add the oil in a steady stream until the mixture becomes thick. Stir in the poppyseeds. Chill several hours before serving.

YIELD: ABOUT 1 CUP

❧ POPPYSEED DRESSING II

This combination is delicious with mixed fruit, but is tart enough to serve on a summer salad of mixed greens.

> *⅓ cup sour cream*
> *1 tablespoon heavy cream*
> *3 tablespoons honey*
> *1 large shallot, minced*
> *1 tablespoon Dijon mustard*
> *2 tablespoons white wine vinegar*
> *2 teaspoons poppyseeds*

Put all the ingredients in a blender and blend until smooth. Serve at once.
YIELD: ABOUT ½ CUP

❧ POPPYSEED DRESSING III

Try this delicious combination on a citrus salad. Even the children will eat it all.

> *¼ cup undiluted frozen lemonade, thawed*
> *⅓ cup honey*
> *¼ cup vegetable oil*
> *1 teaspoon poppyseeds*

Beat all the ingredients together with a whisk in a medium-size mixing bowl. Store in refrigerator if not using immediately.
YIELD: ABOUT 1 CUP

❧ PROVENÇAL DRESSING

Provence, in the south of France, brings to mind visions of seared hills redolent of fresh herbs and wonderful dishes filled with olives, olive oil, and garlic. And, of course, it means tomatoes, eggplant, zucchini—all the best vegetables of summer. Use this fragrant dressing on summer vegetable salads, cold poached fish, or chicken salads.

> 1/4 cup white wine vinegar
> 2 tablespoons fresh lemon juice
> 1 teaspoon honey
> 1 tablespoon Dijon mustard
> Salt and freshly ground black pepper to taste
> 1 1/2 cups olive oil
> 1/2 cup combination of chopped fresh tarragon, thyme, and rosemary

Whisk together the vinegar, lemon juice, honey, mustard, salt, and pepper, then whisk in the oil until the mixture becomes thick. Stir in the herbs. Let stand several hours and beat again before using.

YIELD: ABOUT 2 CUPS

❧ RASPBERRY DRESSING

Raspberry vinegar is one of the most refreshing products of summer. If it is of truly fine quality, it can be spooned into icy cold seltzer water and drunk as a marvelous thirst quencher after a hard day outdoors. Or use it for great dressings like this one. Serve this with summer green salads or over fresh fruit of any kind.

> 3 tablespoons raspberry vinegar
> 1 large shallot, minced
> Salt and freshly ground black pepper to taste
> 1 teaspoon dry white wine
> 1/2 cup olive oil

Whisk together the vinegar, shallot, salt, pepper, and white wine. Beat in olive oil until the mixture becomes thick. Serve at once.

YIELD: ABOUT 1 CUP

❧ RED PEPPER DRESSING

Little more than a tangy puree of red peppers, this dressing is so good on fish salads, you will want to keep it on hand throughout the summer.

> 2 large red bell peppers, roasted until very tender (page 155), skinned, seeded, and chopped
> 1/3 cup olive oil
> 1/4 cup fresh lime juice
> 2 tablespoons white wine vinegar
> 1 large shallot, minced
> 1 clove garlic, minced
> Salt and freshly ground black pepper to taste

Place all the ingredients in a blender and blend until smooth. Let the dressing stand several hours in the refrigerator to develop the flavors. Return to room temperature before serving.

YIELD: ABOUT 3/4 CUP

❧ SESAME SEED DRESSING

There is a definite Oriental flavor to this delightful dressing. The sesame seeds need to be toasted to release the most possible aroma and taste—but be careful not to let them burn. Serve this with green salads, vegetable salads, poultry or cold meat salads. It is also wonderful with cottage cheese and avocado salads.

> 2 tablespoons sesame seeds, spread in one layer in a shallow pan and toasted in a 400°F oven until golden
> 2 tablespoons sesame oil
> 3 tablespoons olive oil
> 2 tablespoons white wine vinegar
> 1 tablespoon grated fresh ginger
> 1 tablespoon light soy sauce
> Freshly ground black pepper to taste

Place the sesame seeds in the bowl of a food processor and pulse until they are ground. With the machine running, add the oils in a thin stream. Add the vinegar, ginger, and soy sauce, and process until smooth. Season with pepper to taste.

YIELD: ABOUT ½ CUP

✲ SPINACH DRESSING

What a beautiful pale green color this dressing is! Especially good with seafood salads, this vinaigrette will also be perfect for any of your favorite pasta salads.

¼ cup chopped fresh spinach
2 tablespoons white wine vinegar
1 tablespoon chopped fresh parsley
2 tablespoons Dijon mustard
1 tablespoon water
½ cup olive oil
Salt and freshly ground black pepper to taste

Place the spinach, vinegar, parsley, mustard, and water in the workbowl of a food processor or blender and puree. With the machine running, add the oil a little at a time until the mixture becomes thick. Season well with salt and pepper. Use at once.

YIELD: ABOUT ⅔ CUP

❧ THYME DRESSING

Why is it the taste of thyme makes us think of long, lazy summer days? This dressing certainly brings back those thoughts and is best served with fresh greens right out of the garden, or sun-ripened tomatoes still warm from the vine.

> 1/3 cup olive oil
> 1 tablespoon chopped fresh thyme
> 2 teaspoons fresh lemon juice
> 1 teaspoon Dijon mustard
> Salt and freshly ground black pepper to taste

Whisk together all the ingredients in a small bowl. Let stand for at least an hour before serving.

YIELD: ABOUT 1/2 CUP

❧ WATERCRESS DRESSING

Watercress has a delicious peppery taste that stands out in this dressing. Look for the freshest watercress, deep green with crisp, resilient stems and leaves without a trace of yellow. Do not use limp greens as they will never taste as good. It would be better to make some other dressing or sauce than compromise. Use this dressing the same day you prepare it.

> 3/4 cup plain yogurt
> 1/4 cup heavy cream
> 1 tablespoon Dijon mustard
> 1 tablespoon white wine vinegar
> 1/4 cup chopped fresh watercress
> 1 clove garlic, minced
> Salt and freshly ground black pepper to taste

Beat together all the ingredients in a medium-size mixing bowl. Chill for an hour or more before serving.

YIELD: ABOUT 1 1/2 CUPS

❧ WINE VINAIGRETTE

The sweet, yeasty taste of this dressing comes from the full-bodied sherry or Madeira. It can stand up to the hearty flavors of fresh spinach, dandelion greens, and vegetables such as zucchini, tomatoes, and eggplant. It is a wonderful summer dressing.

> *⅓ cup Madeira or sherry*
> *2 large egg yolks*
> *2 tablespoons fresh lemon juice*
> *2 tablespoons Dijon mustard*
> *Salt and freshly ground black pepper to taste*
> *1 tablespoon chopped fresh rosemary*
> *⅔ cup olive oil*

Beat together the Madeira, egg yolks, lemon juice, mustard, salt, and pepper in a medium-size mixing bowl. Stir in the rosemary, then whisk in the olive oil, a little at a time, until the dressing thickens. Let the dressing stand for 30 minutes before serving.

YIELD: ABOUT 1¼ CUPS

❧ YOGURT GARLIC DRESSING

Crudités, fresh vegetable salads, and cold poached fish are all greatly enhanced by this tartly delicious sauce. It is quick and easy, and you will want to serve it often. Make it just a few hours before you plan to serve it.

> *¾ cup plain yogurt*
> *2 tablespoons fresh lemon juice*
> *1 clove garlic, minced, or more to taste*
> *3 tablespoons chopped fresh parsley*

Beat together all the ingredients in a medium-size mixing bowl. Chill for about 2 hours before serving.

YIELD: ABOUT 1 CUP

❧ YOGURT WALNUT SAUCE

The pronounced flavor of walnuts is tamed somewhat by the acidic tang of fresh yogurt. Beating the yogurt, much like whipping cream, gives this sauce a very special texture. Serve it with poultry salads, cold poached or baked fish, or with cold steamed shrimp or lobster. While it can be tossed with the other ingredients, it is better when it is spooned onto salads by individual diners. Prepare this dressing on the same day you plan to serve it.

> ¾ cup plain yogurt, beaten with a whisk to stiff peaks
> 2 tablespoons fresh lemon juice
> 2 cloves garlic, minced
> 2 tablespoons chopped walnuts (or more to taste)
> 1 tablespoon chopped fresh mint or basil
> Salt and freshly ground black pepper to taste

Beat the lemon juice into the yogurt in a medium-size mixing bowl. Fold in the remaining ingredients. Refrigerate the dressing several hours, beating once more just before serving.

YIELD: ABOUT 1½ CUPS

CHAPTER FOURTEEN

Fruit Sauces

THIS CHAPTER CONTAINS A MIXTURE OF SWEET AND SAVORY SAUCES. THE common denominator is that they make use of fresh fruits of all kinds. These sauces are especially good when made from the freshest fruit in season. Nothing tastes better than a raspberry sauce made from the first early summer raspberries. After a long, cold winter, those little red globes contain the first promise of summer sun, and the sauce imparts this special flavor to whatever you are serving it with—ice cream, a vanilla soufflé, homemade bread pudding, or a creamy egg custard, still warm from the oven.

The savory sauces based on fruit go very well with heavy meats such as pork or game. While the combination of fruit and meat was anathema in much of Europe until the onset of nouvelle cuisine, both the English and Germans knew how good such dishes could be.

The next time you are in the market, choose the freshest, most beautiful fruit you can find and then turn it into one of these mouthwatering sauces—or substitute one fruit for another, apples for pears, for instance, and create your own special taste.

❦ AMARETTO CHERRY SAUCE

The deep almond taste of amaretto liqueur makes this dessert sauce something special enough for party occasions. Serve it over ice cream, puddings, or even plain cakes. It is also marvelous when spooned over a vanilla soufflé.

> *4 tablespoons (½ stick) butter*
> *½ cup blanched almonds, ground in a blender or food processor*
> *½ cup dark brown sugar*
> *¼ cup heavy cream*
> *¼ cup amaretto liqueur*
> *¾ cup Bing cherries in syrup, drained and pitted*

Melt the butter in a large, heavy saucepan over medium heat. Add the ground almonds, and sauté until they are golden, about 4 to 5 minutes. Stir in the sugar and cream and simmer over low heat for 10 minutes, stirring occasionally. Stir in the amaretto and cherries, and continue cooking until heated through. Serve immediately.

YIELD: ABOUT 1½ CUPS

❦ APPLE AND GINGER SAUCE

This perky sauce goes well with all types of cold meats, especially pork and game. You can store it in the refrigerator for up to two days. Let the sauce return to room temperature before serving.

> *4 large cooking apples, peeled, cored, and sliced*
> *½ cup dry white wine or water*
> *2 tablespoons fresh lemon juice*
> *1 tablespoon grated fresh ginger*
> *¼ cup sugar*
> *1 teaspoon butter*
> *3 tablespoons prepared horseradish, drained*

In a large, heavy saucepan, combine the apples, wine, lemon juice, ginger, and sugar. Simmer over low heat, covered, until the apples are very tender, about 30 minutes. Then remove the cover, increase the heat slightly, and cook until most of the liquid has been reduced to a thick syrup, about 8 to 10 minutes. Add the butter and simmer 1 minute longer, stirring. Remove the sauce from the heat and mash the mixture with a fork until it is smooth. Stir in the horseradish and cool to room temperature before using.

YIELD: ABOUT 2 CUPS

❧ APRICOT SAUCE

Fresh apricots are something that shouldn't be denied to anyone. Used in this delicious dessert sauce, they make even ordinary vanilla ice cream a real treat. Serve it over toasted almond ice cream, and you will have something very good indeed. Fresh summer fruits, sliced and lightly sugared, will also benefit from a little of this fresh-tasting sauce. This sauce can be prepared one day in advance and refrigerated.

1 cup water
15 fresh apricots, halved and stoned
3/4 cup sugar
2 tablespoons fresh lemon juice
1/2 teaspoon vanilla extract

In a large, heavy saucepan, over high heat, bring the water, apricots, and sugar to a boil, then reduce the heat and simmer for 15 minutes. Allow the mixture to cool slightly, then transfer it to a blender or food processor and puree. Let the sauce cool completely before beating in the lemon juice and vanilla. Serve at room temperature.

YIELD: ABOUT 1 1/2 CUPS

❦ BASIC LEMON SAUCE

My childhood memories include sitting at Grandmother's dining room table and being served big squares of just-from-the-oven gingerbread, ready to be split open and smothered with this wonderfully tart-sweet sauce. If it wasn't dripping with sauce, the evening was a total loss. It is still impossible for me to eat gingerbread plain, or even with whipped cream. This lemon sauce is also good with steamed puddings, cakes, and even some fruit desserts, such as tarts and cobblers.

> *½ cup sugar*
> *2 tablespoons cornstarch*
> *Pinch of salt*
> *1 cup water*
> *⅓ cup fresh lemon juice*
> *2 tablespoons grated lemon zest*
> *2 tablespoons (¼ stick) butter*

In a small, heavy saucepan, combine the sugar, cornstarch, salt, and water. Simmer over low heat for 5 minutes, then stir in the lemon juice and zest and simmer 5 minutes longer. Remove the pan from the heat and beat in the butter. Serve immediately, while hot.

YIELD: ABOUT 1 CUP

❦ BLUEBERRY SAUCE

When blueberries are in season, serve them at every meal. No frozen berry will ever have the fragrance or taste that the fresh ones do. This simple and simply delicious sauce is meant for homemade vanilla ice cream, but you can also use it over fresh fruit, any fruit dessert, or with soufflés and mousses. Keep in mind that this sauce needs four hours in the refrigerator before the final preparation can be made, so start it early in the day. It can be prepared up to one day in advance and refrigerated. Rewarm over low heat before serving.

1 pint fresh blueberries, washed and picked over
1/2 cup sugar
1/2 cup sweet white wine or white grape juice
1/4 teaspoon ground cinnamon
1/4 cup brandy
1 teaspoon butter

Reserve ⅓ cup berries and set aside. With a fork, mash the remaining berries in a medium-size mixing bowl with the sugar and wine. Stir in the cinnamon, and let the mixture macerate, covered, in the refrigerator for 4 hours.

Pour the berry mixture into a small, heavy saucepan and bring it to a boil over high heat. Stir in the brandy and simmer the sauce, uncovered, over low heat, for about 15 minutes, until thickened and reduced slightly. Beat in the butter and cook five minutes longer. Cool the sauce slightly and transfer it to a blender or food processor. Puree until smooth. Return the puree to the saucepan and stir in the reserved berries. Heat the sauce through over low heat and serve warm.

YIELD: ABOUT 2 CUPS

❧ BLUEBERRY SAUCE II

This very simple fresh berry sauce is perfect for last-minute suppers when friends drop by unexpectedly. Serve it over vanilla ice cream on slices of buttery pound cake and you have a dessert fit for a king—or queen. Also try it with French toast, pancakes, and waffles. And once you have tasted it with homemade rice pudding, you will never eat it plain again.

1/3 cup sugar
1/2 teaspoon ground cinnamon
2 teaspoons cornstarch
Salt to taste
1 pint blueberries, washed and picked over
1/4 cup fresh lemon juice

In a large, heavy saucepan over medium heat, melt the sugar with the cinnamon, cornstarch, and salt. Stir in the blueberries and cook until the berries pop and the sauce becomes clear. Stir in the lemon juice and serve immediately, while very warm.

YIELD: ABOUT 2 CUPS

❧ BLUEBERRY SAUCE III

This quick sauce uses commercial (or homemade, if you have it) blueberry jelly and can be enjoyed all year long. Serve it with plain cakes, over puddings, with soufflés, or pass it when you have a Grand Marnier soufflé on the menu. This sauce can be prepared one or two days in advance. Rewarm over low heat before serving.

1/2 cup dry red wine
1/2 stick cinnamon
12 whole cloves
1/2 cup sugar
Zest of one lemon
1 tablespoon fresh lemon juice
1/2 cup blueberry jelly

In a medium-size, heavy saucepan, over medium heat, combine the wine, cinnamon, cloves, sugar, zest, and lemon juice. Simmer for 10 minutes, stirring often. Strain through a small sieve. Stir in the blueberry jelly. Simmer for 10 more minutes over very low heat, stirring frequently. Serve hot or warm.

YIELD: ABOUT 1 CUP

❦ CIDER LEMON SAUCE

This variation on the classic lemon sauce is even better than the original. Served in the traditional way, over gingerbread squares, it is strong enough to stand up to even the spiciest preparation. Try it with plain cakes of all kinds, even poppyseed cake, with ice cream, and certainly with old-fashioned bread pudding.

> 1/2 cup sugar
> 1 tablespoon cornstarch
> 1/2 teaspoon ground cinnamon
> 1 cup fresh apple cider, scalded (heated just until bubbles form around edges of pan)
> 2 tablespoons (1/4 stick) butter, softened
> 3 tablespoons fresh lemon juice
> Pinch of salt

In a medium-size, heavy saucepan, over low heat, stir together the sugar, cornstarch, and cinnamon. Slowly beat in the hot cider and simmer 5 minutes, until thick. Remove the sauce from the heat and beat in the butter, lemon juice, and salt. Serve immediately, while warm.

YIELD: ABOUT 1 1/4 CUPS

❧ CRANBERRY CATSUP

Catsup (or ketchup) is probably derived from an ancient Chinese preparation. The idea of a vinegar and onion combination with other ingredients such as tomatoes or fruit, was passed on from China to Malaysia, Indonesia, and India and then to the West. Whenever fresh cranberries are in season, make some of this delicious condiment, pack it in sterilized jars, and serve it all year long with game, roasted or grilled pork, or baked ham.

4 cups fresh or frozen cranberries
2 large onions, minced
1 cup dry white wine
1 cup water
3 cups sugar
2 cups cider vinegar
1 tablespoon ground cinnamon
1 tablespoon ground allspice
1/2 tablespoon ground cloves
1 tablespoon celery seed
1 1/2 teaspoons freshly ground black pepper
1 teaspoon salt
1/2 teaspoon dry mustard

In a large, heavy saucepan, over medium heat, boil the cranberries and onions with the wine and water, until the berries pop. Allow the mixture to cool slightly, then transfer it to a food processor or blender and puree. Return the puree to the saucepan and stir in the remaining ingredients. Simmer over low heat for 30 minutes until thick, stirring occasionally. Pack the boiling catsup into hot, sterilized jars and close tight with new rubber seals and metal rings. Store jars in a cool, dark place. Refrigerate after opening.

YIELD: ABOUT 4 CUPS

❧ CRANBERRY SAUCE

While this fresh cranberry sauce is a delicious accompaniment to holiday turkey, duck, or ham, it can also be used as a dessert sauce over very sweet pastries, cakes, and ice cream. It can be made ahead two or three days and refrigerated until serving time.

> 1 cup fresh or frozen cranberries
> 1/2 cup dry white wine
> 3/4 cup sugar
> 3/4 cup water
> 1/4 cup dark rum
> 2 tablespoons (1/4 stick) butter

In a large, heavy saucepan, over medium heat, combine the cranberries, wine, sugar, and water. Simmer until the berries pop. Stir in the rum and beat in the butter. Serve the sauce hot or chill it until it gels, about 3 hours.

YIELD: 2 1/2 CUPS

❧ FRESH CHERRY SAUCE

Here is a sweet and savory cherry sauce that is excellent with pork, game, and duck when hot. Or serve it hot or cold with cold sliced meats. You can prepare this sauce one day in advance. Store it in the refrigerator and rewarm over low heat before serving.

> 1 pound fresh sweet cherries, washed and stoned
> 2 tablespoons sugar
> 2 tablespoons fresh lemon juice
> 1/4 cup dry white wine
> Pinch of nutmeg
> Red (cayenne) pepper to taste

In a large, heavy saucepan, combine 3/4 of the cherries, the sugar, lemon juice, and white wine. Simmer over low heat for 10 to 15 minutes. Allow the mixture to cool slightly, then transfer it to a food processor or blender and puree. Return the puree to the saucepan, add the remaining cherries, and cook over low heat for 2 minutes. Season with nutmeg and cayenne pepper.

YIELD: ABOUT 1 1/2 CUPS

❧ FRESH STRAWBERRY SAUCE (COULIS DE FRAISES)

This sauce is truly the essence of sweet, ripe strawberries. The sugar, lemon juice, and rum only enhance their pure natural flavor. Serve it over the freshest of fruit—and for a double treat, pour it over fresh hulled strawberries.

> 1 pint fresh strawberries, hulled and sliced
> 1/2 cup sugar
> 1 tablespoon fresh lemon juice
> 2 tablespoons dark rum
> 1/2 teaspoon finely chopped candied ginger (optional)

In a blender, puree the strawberries, sugar, and lemon juice until smooth. Stir in the rum and ginger if using. Refrigerate at least one hour, and serve within a few hours.

YIELD: ABOUT 1 CUP

❧ LEMON CREAM SAUCE

Serve this delicious savory sauce with cooked vegetables of all kinds. It is especially wonderful with freshly steamed asparagus, and makes a boiled artichoke something very special indeed.

> 1/2 cup Chicken Stock (page 12)
> 1/2 cup dry white wine
> 1 tablespoon grated fresh ginger
> 1 tablespoon grated lemon zest
> 1 tablespoon fresh lemon juice
> 3/4 cup heavy cream
> Salt and freshly ground white pepper to taste

In a small, heavy saucepan, over high heat, boil the stock, wine, ginger, zest, and lemon juice until reduced to 1/2 cup, about 10 minutes. Stir in the cream and cook over high heat until reduced further to 3/4 cup of sauce, about 15 minutes more. Season with salt and pepper and serve immediately.

YIELD: ABOUT 3/4 CUP

❦ GINGERED PEAR SAUCE

While this makes an excellent hot dessert sauce, especially over bread pudding, gingerbread, spice cake, and ice cream (try it with rum raisin!), it is also delicious when served at room temperature with cold roasted meats. If desired, this sauce can be prepared up to two days in advance and refrigerated.

> 3 large pears, peeled, cored, and cut into chunks
> 1/2 cup sugar
> 3 tablespoons minced candied ginger
> 1 tablespoon fresh lemon juice
> 1 teaspoon grated lemon zest
> 1/2 teaspoon vanilla extract

In a large, heavy saucepan, over medium heat, simmer the pears with water to cover over low heat for 20 minutes. Drain and transfer the pears to a food processor or blender and puree. Return the pears to the saucepan and add the sugar, ginger, lemon juice, and zest. Simmer for 10 minutes over medium heat, stirring from time to time. Remove the sauce from the heat and beat in the vanilla.

YIELD: ABOUT 1 CUP

❧ MELBA SAUCE

This sauce may or may not have been developed for the famous Nellie Melba. However it came to be, it is a delicious addition to ice cream, fruit, or pastries.

> 1 cup fresh raspberries, washed and picked over
> 1/2 cup sugar
> 1/2 cup red currant jelly
> 1 tablespoon cornstarch
> 2 tablespoons water

In a large, heavy saucepan, over medium heat, combine the berries, sugar, and jelly. Mash the berries thoroughly with a fork and simmer gently for 5 minutes. Mix the cornstarch with the water in a small bowl to form a smooth paste, then stir into the berry mixture. Cook the mixture, over low heat, stirring until the sauce is smooth and clear, about 3 minutes. Cool to warm or room temperature and serve immediately.

YIELD: ABOUT 1 1/4 CUPS

❧ ORANGE CREAM SAUCE

The cream in this rich, delicious sauce makes it a natural over all kinds of cakes, soufflés, puddings, and even ice cream.

> 1 1/2 cups heavy cream
> 1/2 cup sugar
> 1/2 cup fresh orange juice
> 1 tablespoon fresh lemon juice
> 1/4 cup grated orange zest
> 2 tablespoons (1/4 stick) butter
> 2 tablespoons Grand Marnier or other orange liqueur

In a large, heavy saucepan, cook the cream over high heat until reduced by half, at least 10 to 15 minutes. Then, over low heat, dissolve the sugar in the hot cream. Stir in the orange juice, lemon juice, and zest until combined. Beat in the butter and orange liqueur. Heat through and serve immediately.

YIELD: ABOUT 2 CUPS

❧ ORANGE SAUCE

Pour this refreshing sauce over fresh fruit or slices of plain cake. It can be prepared two to three days in advance. Rewarm over low heat, if desired.

> *¹/₂ cup sugar*
> *¹/₂ cup orange juice*
> *4 tablespoons (¹/₂ stick) butter, softened*
> *1 tablespoon grated lemon zest*
> *1 tablespoon fresh lemon juice*
> *¹/₄ cup brandy*

Combine all the ingredients in a small, heavy saucepan and beat over low heat until smooth, about 4 to 5 minutes. Serve hot or cold.

YIELD: ABOUT 1 CUP

❧ ORANGE SAUCE II

This is a variation of the original hot lemon sauce. It is slightly less tart and can be served with ice cream.

> *1 cup orange juice*
> *¹/₂ cup sugar*
> *2 tablespoons cornstarch*
> *1 teaspoon grated fresh ginger*
> *¹/₄ cup fresh lemon juice*
> *1 tablespoon rum*

Blend the orange juice, sugar, cornstarch, and ginger in a small, heavy saucepan. Simmer over high heat until thickened, about 3 minutes. Stir in the lemon juice and rum and continue cooking until heated through. Serve immediately, while still warm.

YIELD: ABOUT 1 ¹/₂ CUPS

❧ PEACH CHUTNEY

While most of us are familiar with mango chutney, it is very simple to make this sweetly delicious variation. Serve it with any kind of curry, beef stew, roasted pork, lamb, or any kind of cold cut, especially ham.

2 1/2 pounds peaches, peeled, stoned, and sliced
1 1/2 cups cider vinegar
2 cups firmly packed dark brown sugar
1/2 small onion, finely chopped
1 1/2 cups seedless raisins
2 apples, peeled, cored, and chopped
2 teaspoons pickling spices
Zest of one lemon, grated
1/4 cup fresh lemon juice

Combine the peaches, vinegar, and sugar in a large, heavy kettle. Simmer over low heat until the peaches are slightly tender, about 15 minutes. Add the remaining ingredients and simmer until thickened, like preserves, about 15 to 20 minutes.

Pack the boiling chutney in hot, sterilized jars and close tightly with new rubber seals and metal rings, or refrigerate. If canned, store jars in a cool, dark, place. Refrigerate after jar is opened. Serve at room temperature.

YIELD: ABOUT 4 CUPS

❧ PEACH CREAM SAUCE

This fresh peach sauce enriched with cream is wonderful with homemade vanilla ice cream served in cookie cups.

4 large peaches, peeled, stoned, and chopped
1 cup water
1/4 cup sugar
Pinch of ground cinnamon
1/2 cup heavy cream
1 tablespoon butter
1 teaspoon almond extract

In a large saucepan, over medium heat, simmer the peaches, water, sugar, and cinnamon until the peaches are very tender, about 20 minutes. Transfer the mixture to a blender or food processor and puree. Return the puree to the saucepan and beat in the cream, butter, and almond extract. Simmer over very low heat until thick and smooth, about 5 minutes more. Serve hot or cold. Use at once.

YIELD: ABOUT 2 CUPS

❦ PEACH SAUCE

Ripe summer peaches are wonderful, no matter how you eat them. Make them doubly delicious when you serve them sliced and topped with this delicious fresh sauce. Any combination of summer fruit will be better with this sauce, and you can also use it for topping cakes or fruited bread pudding.

> *4 medium-size peaches, peeled and stoned*
> *¼ cup light corn syrup*
> *¼ cup sugar*
> *1 tablespoon cornstarch*
> *1 tablespoon water*
> *2 tablespoons rum*

In a large, heavy saucepan, over low heat, simmer the peaches in water to cover for 10 minutes. Then drain and puree them in a food processor or blender. Return the puree to the saucepan, raise the heat to medium, and add the corn syrup and sugar. Stir the cornstarch and water together in a small bowl until dissolved. Then stir the cornstarch mixture into the puree and bring it to a boil over high heat.

Remove the sauce from the heat and stir in the rum. Cool to room temperature and serve immediately.

YIELD: ABOUT 1¼ CUPS

❧ RAISIN DESSERT SAUCE

Anything with raisins in it was an immediate hit with my father. This sauce would be high on his list of good things, especially if it were poured over a freshly baked rice or bread pudding.

> 2 large egg yolks
> 1/3 cup firmly packed dark brown sugar
> 1 teaspoon cornstarch
> 1 teaspoon grated lemon zest
> 3 tablespoons cream sherry
> 1/3 cup golden raisins plumped in 1/4 cup hot rum for 10 minutes and drained

Whisk together the egg yolks, brown sugar, cornstarch, zest, and sherry in a medium-size, heavy saucepan until frothy. Then simmer the mixture over very low heat until it is thick and clear, at least several minutes. Stir the raisins into the sauce and serve immediately.

YIELD: ABOUT 1 CUP

❧ RASPBERRY SAUCE

Fruit salads, sorbets, and ice creams will be made even better with this very fresh raspberry sauce.

> 2 cups fresh raspberries, pureed and sieved to remove seeds
> 1/4 cup sugar
> 1 tablespoon cornstarch
> 2 tablespoons fresh lemon juice
> 1/4 cup water
> 2 tablespoons brandy
> 1 tablespoon dark rum

Combine the raspberry puree, sugar, cornstarch, lemon juice, and water in a large, heavy saucepan. Simmer, stirring, over low heat, until thick, about 3 minutes. Stir in the brandy and dark rum and serve at once, very hot.

YIELD: ABOUT 1 CUP

❧ SAVORY BLACK CURRANT SAUCE

Here is a savory black currant sauce that makes a lovely accompaniment to duck, pork, and game. This sauce can be made several hours ahead of time. Rewarm it over low heat before serving.

> *2 tablespoons (1/4 stick) butter*
> *3 large shallots, minced*
> *2 cloves garlic, minced*
> *1/4 cup brandy*
> *1/2 cup black currant jelly*
> *1/4 cup Dijon mustard*
> *1/4 cup dry white wine*
> *Salt and freshly ground black pepper to taste*

Melt the butter in a medium-size heavy saucepan over medium heat. Add the shallots and garlic and sauté until transparent, about 3 to 5 minutes. Stir in the brandy, jelly, mustard, and wine, and simmer over low heat for 10 minutes. Season with salt and pepper. Serve warm.

YIELD: ABOUT 1 CUP

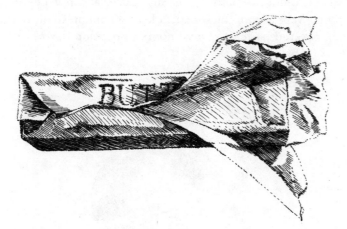

❧ SAVORY PLUM SAUCE

The fruity flavor of this complex sauce goes perfectly with roasted chicken, charcoal-grilled duck breast, or with a spit-roasted loin of pork. You can also baste the Easter ham with it for a very special treat. This sauce keeps for a week or two in the refrigerator.

> *1 tablespoon vegetable oil*
> *2 cups Sweet Plum Sauce (see following recipe)*
> *1 teaspoon Chinese five spice powder (a combination of ground anise, cinnamon, fennel, cloves, and black pepper, available in Asian groceries)*
> *1 teaspoon ground cumin*
> *½ teaspoon dry mustard*
> *1 large onion, chopped*
> *½ cup tomato sauce (see Index)*
> *1 tablespoon light soy sauce*
> *Hot pepper sauce to taste*
> *2 tablespoons rice or white wine vinegar*

Heat the oil in a large, heavy saucepan over low heat. Stir in the plum sauce, spices, onion, tomato sauce, soy sauce, and hot pepper sauce. Simmer, uncovered, until thickened, at least 30 minutes. Stir in the vinegar. Chill, covered, at least several hours to develop flavors.

YIELD: ABOUT 2½ CUPS

❧ SWEET PLUM SAUCE

Use this fruity sauce over fruit salad and ice cream. It is also excellent as a base for more complex sauces, such the Savory Plum Sauce on page 228. This sauce can be stored for up to two days in the refrigerator. Allow it to return to room temperature before serving.

1 ½ pounds plums, pitted and quartered
¼ cup sweet white wine
¼ cup water
½ cup sugar
1 teaspoon chopped fresh ginger

In a large, heavy saucepan, combine the plums, wine, and water. Cover and simmer until soft, about 10 to 15 minutes. Stir in the sugar and ginger and simmer until the fruit falls apart, about another 15 minutes or more, depending on the fruits' size and ripeness. Beat the sauce until smooth and serve at room temperature.

YIELD: ABOUT 2 CUPS

CHAPTER FIFTEEN

❧ *Sweet Sauces*

WAS THERE EVER A DESSERT THAT DID NOT BENEFIT FROM A SAUCE? EVEN THE most mundane bowl of ice cream becomes something special when topped with a homemade sweet sauce. Some of the most heavenly dessert sauces are those made of custard and I have included several in this section.

Custard sauces can be made in all flavors—vanilla, chocolate mint, raspberry, lemon—or any other that suits your whim. However, they are the only sweet sauces that do require a little care. So, take the time to read the following tips as well as those that follow concerning chocolate.

SWEET SAUCE TIPS

- Because custard sauces are based on eggs, the old problem of curdling from overheating raises its ugly head. But if you know how to handle the eggs correctly, your sauce will escape uncurdled and silky smooth.

  Just follow this basic method. First, beat the eggs with the sugar. Then, scald the milk or cream until bubbles begin to form around the edges. Remove it from the burner and delicately whisk a little of the hot liquid into the eggs in order to cook them slightly. Then beat the egg mixture back into the hot milk and stir your custard over low heat until it begins to thicken.

  Finally, to prevent the sauce from curdling while it cools, and to eliminate any egg that may have solidified during the cooking, it is a good idea to strain the custard through a fine sieve into a clean bowl. Custards can be served hot, at room temperature, or chilled.

- The only other thing you must remember is to keep stirring! The custard must be stirred constantly to prevent the bottom from becoming too hot. The traditional way to stir a custard is with a wooden spoon, using a figure eight pattern, which is supposed to cover the entire bottom of the pan. Once the custard begins to thicken, remove it from the heat and let it cool.

- Chocolate also requires a little care. If melting it alone, take care not to stir very often. Chocolate burns or clumps up if too much heat is applied to it. There are several ways to melt chocolate without this happening. If liquid is used in the recipe, melt the chocolate in the liquid over low heat, stirring constantly. Or, melt the chocolate in the microwave if you have one. Place chocolate in a 4-cup glass measure. Cook at medium low for 3 minutes or until melted. Or follow the manufacturer's instructions. You can also place the chocolate in the top of a double boiler over barely simmering (not boiling) water, or melt it directly in a saucepan over very low heat, stirring constantly until the chocolate is almost liquid. Then remove the pan from the heat and stir to finish melting.

- Use the type of chocolate (bittersweet, semi-sweet, white, etc.) called for in each recipe. And, yes, quality does matter. The better the chocolate, the better the sauce. Luckily, some brands you can find in the supermarket, such as Baker's, will fit the bill for many of the chocolate sauces in this section.

❧ BROWN SUGAR SAUCE

Adapted from an old Virginia recipe, this sweet, rich sauce makes butter-scotch from a jar look insipid. Spoon it over ice cream and pound cake, gingerbread, bread pudding, rice pudding, or vanilla soufflés.

> 4 tablespoons (½ stick) butter, softened
> 2 cups firmly packed dark brown sugar
> 2 large eggs
> ¼ cup heavy cream
> 3 tablespoons bourbon
> 1 teaspoon vanilla extract

Cream together the butter and sugar in a large mixing bowl until light and fluffy. Add the eggs and beat until smooth. Beat in the cream, then transfer the mixture to the top of a double boiler, and cook over barely simmering water for one hour, beating every 15 or 20 minutes. The finished sauce should be very thick and creamy.

Remove the sauce from the heat and beat in the bourbon and vanilla. Serve immediately, while hot.

YIELD: ABOUT 1½ CUPS

❧ BUTTERSCOTCH SAUCE

This classic butterscotch still makes one of the most wonderful sundaes that will ever pass your lips. It can be made up to two days in advance and refrigerated.

> ⅓ cup light corn syrup
> 2 tablespoons (¼ stick) butter
> ¾ cup firmly packed dark brown sugar
> ½ teaspoon fresh lemon juice
> ¼ cup heavy cream

In a small, heavy saucepan, over medium heat, combine the corn syrup, butter, and brown sugar, and boil for 5 to 7 minutes. Remove the sauce from the heat and beat in the lemon juice and cream. Serve hot or cold.

YIELD: ABOUT 1 CUP

❦ CARAMEL CUSTARD SAUCE

Custards are sometimes tricky. Too much heat can cook the egg yolks and the end result is somewhat like sweetened scrambled eggs. Even if you sieve the sauce, it cannot be made smooth again. So you must take care not to overheat any sauce that contains egg yolks. Caramelized sugar is also delicate. Since it burns all too easily, watch it closely. As soon as it has reached the desired golden brown, remove it from the heat at once. Serve this luscious sauce with fruit, ice cream, and cakes of all kinds. It can be prepared up to one day in advance. Beat well before serving.

½ cup plus 2 tablespoons sugar
½ cup water
3 large egg yolks
*1 cup milk, scalded (heated just until bubbles form around edges of pan) and
    kept hot*
1 teaspoon vanilla extract

Simmer ½ cup of the sugar and the water in a small, heavy saucepan over medium heat until the sugar has dissolved and the mixture has just turned golden brown, about 10 to 15 minutes. Watch carefully to make sure it doesn't burn and do not stir or else the mixture will crystallize.

Meanwhile, beat together the remaining two tablespoons of sugar and the eggs yolks in a small bowl. Beat ¼ cup of the hot syrup into the eggs, then beat the eggs into the hot milk. Simmer the mixture over low heat, stirring, until it has thickened, about 8 to 10 minutes, but do not allow it to boil.

Remove it from the heat and stir in the rest of the hot caramel. If the caramel hardens in the milk, keep stirring until it has completely melted. Beat in the vanilla. Serve warm or cold.

YIELD: ABOUT 1 CUP

❦ CHERRY CHOCOLATE SAUCE

There is hardly room in this book to list all the things you can put this lovely chocolate sauce on. But just in case you haven't thought of it, it's delicious on top of waffles, pancakes, or French toast, and fabulous with ice cream and freshly made pound cake. This sauce can be stored for three days in the refrigerator.

> 1/2 cup sugar
> 1/4 cup unsweetened cocoa powder
> 1/2 cup half and half
> 1/3 cup light corn syrup
> 4 tablespoons (1/2 stick) butter
> Pinch of salt
> 2 ounces (2 squares) unsweetened chocolate
> 2 teaspoons vanilla extract
> 1 tablespoon kirsch

In a small, heavy saucepan, over medium heat, combine the sugar and cocoa, mixing well. Stir in the half and half, corn syrup, butter, chocolate, and salt. Cook the mixture stirring constantly, until it comes to a boil and becomes smooth. Remove the sauce from the heat and stir in the vanilla and kirsch. Serve hot.

YIELD: ABOUT 1 1/2 CUPS

❧ CHOCOLATE CUSTARD SAUCE

Custard sauces are perfect with mousses, soufflés, and freshly poached meringues. Some fruits even go well with custards. Serve this one with a Grand Marnier soufflé, orange pound cake, or bread pudding. I even know one chocolate nut who thinks it's a great drink.

> ⅔ cup sugar
> ¼ cup unsweetened cocoa powder
> Pinch of salt
> 3 large eggs, beaten
> 2 cups half and half or milk, scalded (heated just until bubbles form around
>   edges of pan) and kept hot
> 1 tablespoon brandy

Stir together the sugar, cocoa, and salt in a large mixing bowl. Beat in the eggs until creamy. Beat ¼ cup of the hot half and half into the egg mixture, then beat all of the egg mixture into the remaining cream. Cook the sauce over low heat, stirring constantly, until thickened, about 8 to 10 minutes. Remove it from heat and stir in the brandy. Strain the sauce through a small sieve if desired. Serve immediately or chill and serve within a few hours.

YIELD: ABOUT 2 CUPS

❧ CHOCOLATE FONDUE

For anyone who loves a good cheese fondue, this sauce will provide another dipping experience. This fondue sauce is normally served with squares of buttery rich pound cake or the freshest of fruits—lush, ripe strawberries, large chunks of fresh pineapple, quarters of ripe pears. Simply spear the fruit or cake, dip it in this warm chocolate, and enjoy.

> ⅔ cup light corn syrup
> ½ cup heavy cream
> 8 ounces semisweet chocolate, broken into small pieces

In a medium-size, heavy saucepan, over medium heat, bring the corn syrup and cream to a boil. Remove the pan from the heat and beat in the chocolate until it is melted. Serve immediately, while hot.

YIELD: ABOUT 1½ CUPS

❧ CHOCOLATE MINT SAUCE

Chocolate and mint have a special affinity, and those who love that combination will love this sauce, as well. Spoon it over vanilla or chocolate ice cream, white chocolate mousse, cakes of all kinds—even over waffles, pancakes, and French toast! You can prepare this sauce up to two days in advance and store it in the refrigerator. Rewarm it over low heat before serving.

> *4 ounces semisweet chocolate, chopped*
> *2 tablespoons (¼ stick) butter*
> *½ cup sugar*
> *1 cup heavy cream*
> *1 teaspoon peppermint extract (or more to taste)*

Melt the chocolate in a double boiler over simmering, but not boiling, water. Add the butter and sugar, stir in the cream, then place the pot directly over low heat and simmer for 5 minutes. Remove the sauce from the heat and beat in the extract. Serve warm.

YIELD: ABOUT 1 CUP

❧ COFFEE CUSTARD SAUCE

Fill warm, freshly made crepes with white chocolate mousse and smother them with some of this custard sauce for a dessert to remember. Or, spoon some onto a dessert plate and arrange balls of deep chocolate mousse on top. Add a candied coffee bean and watch your guests' eyes light up. It is equally good with cakes, some fruit desserts (shortcakes or fresh fruit salad), and, of course, freshly poached meringues.

> *1 tablespoon instant coffee or instant espresso, or more to taste*
> *1½ cups half and half, boiled over high heat until reduced to 1 cup, and kept warm*
> *3 tablespoons sugar*
> *2 large egg yolks*
> *1 tablespoon brandy*

Dissolve the instant coffee in the hot cream and set aside. Beat together the sugar and egg yolks in a small bowl until light and fluffy. Beat in ¼ cup of the hot cream, then beat all of the egg mixture back into the remaining cream and cook over low heat until thickened, about 8 to 10 minutes.

Remove the sauce from the heat, stir in brandy, and strain through a small sieve, if desired. Serve immediately, or chill and serve within a few hours.

YIELD: ABOUT 1 CUP

❧ CRÈME ANGLAISE (VANILLA CUSTARD SAUCE)

This is the one that started it all. This delicious custard sauce is the most all-purpose dessert sauce in this book. Serve it with virtually anything, from fresh fruit to double-rich chocolate cake.

4 large egg yolks, beaten
⅓ cup sugar
Pinch of salt
2 cups milk, half and half, or heavy cream, scalded (heated just until bubbles
*   form around edges of pan) and kept warm*
1 teaspoon vanilla extract

Beat the egg yolks with the sugar and salt in a large mixing bowl until light and foamy. Gradually beat the hot milk into the egg yolks, then place the bowl over hot water or transfer the mixture to the top of a double boiler over barely simmering water. Cook, stirring constantly, until the mixture coats a spoon, as long as 8 minutes. Remove the sauce from the heat and strain it through a sieve. Stir in the vanilla and allow the sauce to cool. Serve it within a few hours, cold or at room temperature.

YIELD: ABOUT 2 CUPS

❧ CUSTARD SAUCE

This version of a custard sauce is less rich than any of the others. The addition of a little cornstarch makes it smoother, but it is still quite nice, especially over fresh fruit, with a chocolate soufflé, or with any kind of fudge cake.

> ½ cup sugar
> 2 tablespoons cornstarch
> 2 large egg yolks
> 1 cup half and half, scalded (heated just until bubbles form around edges of pan) and kept warm
> 2 teaspoons vanilla extract

Beat together the sugar, cornstarch, and egg yolks in a small bowl. Beat a ¼ cup of the hot half and half into the egg yolk mixture, then stir the egg yolk mixture into the remaining half and half. Simmer the sauce over low heat, stirring constantly, until thickened, as long as 8 minutes. Remove the sauce from the heat and stir in the vanilla. Serve immediately or chill and serve within a few hours.

YIELD: ABOUT 1 CUP

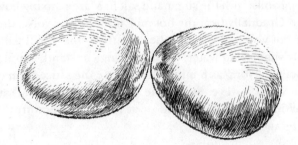

❧ ELEGANT SABAYON

Creamy, light, and as elegant as its name, this egg yolk sauce is delicious eaten by itself, with broken up macaroons stirred into it, over cakes, puddings, mousses, or fruit.

> 4 large egg yolks
> 1/3 cup sugar
> 3/4 cup sparkling wine

With a wire whisk, beat together all the ingredients in a medium-size, round-bottomed, heavy saucepan over very low heat until thick and foamy, about 10 minutes. Serve at once.

YIELD: ABOUT 1 1/2 CUPS

❧ GINGER CUSTARD SAUCE

Of all the custards, this one is the best served over fresh fruit. There is something about the spiciness of the ginger that makes the combination unforgettable. This custard can be prepared up to two days in advance and refrigerated until serving.

> 1 cup half and half or milk, scalded (heated just until bubbles form around
>   edges of pan)
> 3 tablespoons minced candied ginger
> 1/3 cup sugar
> 2 large egg yolks
> 1 teaspoon vanilla extract

In a small, heavy saucepan, over low heat, simmer the scalded half and half and ginger for 3 minutes. Meanwhile, beat together the eggs and sugar in a small bowl until light. Beat in 1/4 cup of the half and half, then beat all of the egg mixture back into the remaining cream. Cook over low heat, stirring constantly, until the mixture coats the back of a spoon, about 5 to 8 minutes. Do not allow the mixture to boil—the eggs will curdle. Remove the sauce from the heat and stir in the vanilla. Chill and beat well before serving.

YIELD: ABOUT 1 CUP

❦ HARD SAUCE

This cold sauce is served on hot desserts in both Great Britain and the United States. Make it at least one day ahead so that the flavors have a chance to develop. Serve it with steamed puddings, such as the traditional Christmas plum pudding, with fruit cakes (the richer and darker, the better), or with bread pudding that is stuffed with raisins. This sauce will keep for up to one month in the refrigerator, but don't freeze it.

> 1 1/4 cups confectioners' sugar
> 1/4 cup brandy
> 1/4 pound (1 stick) unsalted butter, softened

In a large mixing bowl, beat the sugar and brandy into the butter, a little at a time. When the mixture is smooth, spoon into a serving dish and chill. Serve cold.

YIELD: ABOUT 1 CUP

❦ HOT BRANDY SAUCE

Here is another Southern favorite. It is exceptionally good with steamed puddings, but it also holds its own with ice creams and cakes of all kinds. If desired, this sauce can be prepared up to two days in advance and stored in the refrigerator.

> 1 cup sugar
> 1/4 cup water
> 1/2 cup heavy cream
> 1/3 cup brandy
> 1 tablespoon butter

In a large, heavy saucepan, dissolve the sugar in the water. Cook over low heat until dissolved, then simmer until the sugar is a golden syrup. Do not stir or the mixture will crystallize. As soon as the mixture has turned golden, stir in the cream very carefully, since the mixture may foam up. Simmer over low heat for 2 minutes. Stir in the brandy and heat the sauce through. Then remove the sauce from the heat and beat in the butter. Serve hot or cold.

YIELD: ABOUT 1/2 CUP

❧ MAPLE SYRUP AND WALNUT SAUCE

If maple syrup is one of your favorites, you will love this very New England sauce. It is very sweet, but adds punch to plain ice cream, cakes, and puddings, or a vanilla soufflé. This sauce will keep for up to two days in the refrigerator. Rewarm it over low heat before serving, if desired.

> ¾ cup pure maple syrup
> ¼ cup heavy cream (optional)
> ½ cup coarsely chopped walnuts

In a small, heavy saucepan, over medium heat, cook the syrup for about 8 minutes, or until it begins to thicken. Remove it from the heat and beat in the cream (if you're using it) and walnuts. Serve warm.

YIELD: ABOUT 1 CUP

❧ OLD-FASHIONED HOT FUDGE SAUCE

Anything—ANYTHING—that goes with chocolate will be perfect with this sauce. It will keep for up to a week in the refrigerator.

> 4 ounces (4 squares) unsweetened chocolate
> One 12-ounce can evaporated milk
> 2½ cups confectioners' sugar
> Pinch of salt
> 2 teaspoons vanilla extract
> 3 tablespoons butter

In the top of a double boiler, combine the chocolate, milk, sugar, and salt, and cook over simmering, not boiling, water until the chocolate is melted and smooth. Remove the sauce from the heat and beat in the vanilla and butter. Serve hot or cold.

YIELD: ABOUT 2 CUPS

❧ ORANGE CHOCOLATE SAUCE

Orange and chocolate are two favorite flavors that were made for each other. Use this sauce to top cakes, ice cream, mousses, and puddings. It can be prepared up to two days in advance and stored in the refrigerator. Rewarm it over low heat before serving.

> *4 ounces semisweet chocolate*
> *2 tablespoons (1/4 stick) butter*
> *1/2 cup sugar*
> *1 tablespoon grated orange zest*
> *2/3 cup heavy cream*
> *3 tablespoons Grand Marnier or other orange liqueur*

Melt the chocolate in the top of a double boiler over simmering, not boiling, water. Stir in the butter, sugar, zest, and cream, and simmer for 2 to 3 minutes. Remove the sauce from the heat and stir in the Grand Marnier. Serve warm.

YIELD: ABOUT 1 CUP

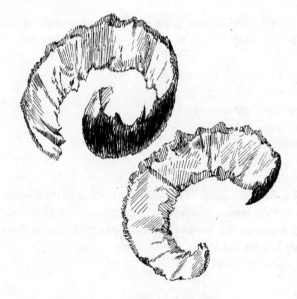

❧ PRALINE SAUCE

In New Orleans there are two schools of thought about pralines. Some are adamant that there be no cream in the candy, others are just as sure that cream is an essential ingredient.

This sauce belongs to the latter school. It is creamy and full of the goodness of brown sugar and pecans. Serve it over ice cream, cakes—especially rich, buttery pound cake—puddings, and other sweets.

4 tablespoons (½ stick) butter
¾ cup firmly packed dark brown sugar
⅓ cup dark corn syrup
1 cup heavy cream, boiled over high heat until reduced to ½ cup
1 teaspoon vanilla extract
1 cup chopped pecans, toasted

Stir together the butter, brown sugar, and corn syrup in a large, heavy saucepan and simmer for about 5 minutes over low heat until the butter and the sugar melt and the mixture becomes smooth. Remove the sauce from the heat and beat in the cream and vanilla. Stir in the pecans. Serve immediately, while hot.

YIELD: ABOUT 2 CUPS

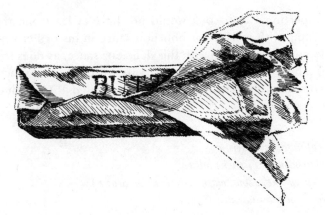

❧ SABAYON SAUCE

Instead of being made with sparkling wine, like Elegant Sabayon on page 239, this one is very Italian in nature—containing marsala—and is delicious eaten by itself right off the stove. However, it's best with fresh, sweet, ripe strawberries.

> ½ cup superfine granulated sugar
> 1 cup marsala, sweet sherry, or Madeira
> 5 large egg yolks, beaten

In the top of a double boiler, beat together the sugar and wine, then beat in egg yolks. Place the mixture over simmering, not boiling, water and beat with a whisk until thick, about 5 to 7 minutes. Remove the sauce from the heat and continue to beat until cool. Serve warm or cold within a few hours.

YIELD: ABOUT 2 CUPS

❧ WHISKEY SAUCE

No self-respecting Cajun cook would not have at least one recipe for bread pudding with whiskey or bourbon sauce in his or her repertoire. Rice pudding also goes well with this delicious sauce, as does ice cream. Or spoon a little over plain cake for an instant treat. This sauce can be prepared up to four days in advance and refrigerated. Rewarm it over low heat before serving.

> ½ cup light corn syrup
> 2 tablespoons (¼ stick) butter
> ¼ cup whiskey (sour mash, bourbon, or Scotch)
> 1 teaspoon vanilla extract

In a small, heavy saucepan, over medium heat, bring the corn syrup to a boil. Remove the pan from the heat and beat in the butter, whiskey, and vanilla. Serve warm.

YIELD: ABOUT ⅔ CUP

WHITE CHOCOLATE SAUCE

This sauce will become a favorite, especially with chocolate cake, chocolate mousse, fruit mousses, or fresh fruit. It is easy and quick and very appealing.

> ¼ cup sugar
> 1 ½ cups heavy cream, boiled over high heat until reduced to 1 cup
> 1 teaspoon vanilla extract
> 2 tablespoons brandy
> 6 ounces white chocolate, broken into pieces

In a medium-size, heavy saucepan, combine the sugar and cream and simmer over medium heat until the liquid has been reduced by half. Remove the pan from the heat and stir in the vanilla and brandy. Beat in the chocolate until it is fully melted and the sauce is smooth. Serve immediately.

YIELD: ABOUT 1 ½ CUPS

❧ *Recipes by Food Category*

❧ SAUCES FOR BEEF

Basic Red Wine Sauce
Beurre Rouge
Blue Cheese Brandy Butter
Bordelaise Sauce
Classic Mushroom Sauce
Easy Béarnaise
Espagnole Sauce
Fruity Marinade
Garlic and Honey Marinade
Herb Sauce
Hot Horseradish Sauce
Hot Tomato Sauce
Lemon Barbecue Sauce
Lyonnaise Sauce
Maître d'Hôtel Butter
Mustard Shallot Butter
Pepper Sauce (Poivrade)
Pico de Gallo
Port Wine Sauce
Ravigote Sauce (Cold)
Ravigote Sauce (Hot)
Red Wine Marinade

❧ SAUCES FOR DESSERTS

Basic Lemon Sauce
Blueberry Sauce
Brown Sugar Sauce
Butterscotch Sauce
Caramel Custard Sauce
Chocolate Custard Sauce
Chocolate Fondue
Coffee Custard Sauce
Crème Anglaise
Custard Sauce
Elegant Sabayon
Ginger Custard Sauce
Hot Brandy Sauce
Old-fashioned Hot Fudge Sauce
Orange Butter
Orange Sauce
Praline Sauce
Raisin Sauce
Sabayon Sauce
Sweet Plum Sauce
Whiskey Sauce
White Chocolate Sauce

❦ SAUCES FOR EGGS

Aioli
Anchovy Butter
Aurore Sauce
Basic Red Wine Sauce
Beurre Rouge
Blender Hollandaise
Bonne Femme Sauce
Classic Hollandaise
Crab Sauce
Creamy Curry Sauce
Creamy Mustard Sauce
Creole Sauce
Eggplant Sauce
Herb Sauce
Hot Horseradish Sauce
Lemon Mustard Sauce
Lyonnaise Sauce
Mint Hollandaise
Mornay Sauce
Mousseline Sauce
Ravigote Sauce
Ravigote Sauce (Hot)
Rustic Tomato Sauce
Sauce Nantua
South American Cheese Sauce
Tuna Sauce
Velouté

❦ SAUCES FOR FISH

Aioli
Anchovy Butter
Anchovy Mayonnaise
Anchovy Sauce
Aurore Sauce

Avgolemono
Avocado Butter
Avocado Sauce
Basic Red Wine Sauce
Basil Mayonnaise
Basil Sauce
Bercy
Beurre Blanc
Beurre Rouge
Black Pepper Butter
Blender Hollandaise
Bonne Femme Sauce
Butter Herb Sauce
Carlton Butter
Chipotle Sauce
Choron Sauce
Classic Hollandaise
Cold Curry Sauce
Cold Mustard Sauce
Cold Yogurt Sauce
Creamy Curry Sauce
Creamy Mustard Sauce
Creole Sauce
Cucumber Sauce
Dijon Yogurt Dressing
Double Mustard Sauce
Easy Béarnaise
Easy Tomato Sauce
Egg Sauce
Fresh Tomato Sauce
Fresh Vegetable Salsa
Fresh Vegetable Sauce
Fruity Salsa
Garlic Sauce
Garlic Basil Butter
Garlic Butter
Ginger Sauce
Greek Tsatsiki
Green Mayonnaise
Green Onion Sauce

Green Peppercorn Butter
Green Salsa
Grill Sauce
Ham and Walnut Sauce
Hazelnut Butter Sauce
Herb Butter
Herbed Avocado Sauce
Honey Soy Basting Sauce
Horseradish Dill Sauce
Hot Tomato Sauce
Leek and Tomato Sauce
Lemon Mayonnaise
Lemon Mustard Sauce
Lemon Wine Sauce
Lime Basting Sauce
Lime and Pepper Butter
Lime Butter
Machine Mint Mayonnaise
Maître d'Hôtel Butter
Marinara Sauce
Middle Eastern Eggplant Sauce
Mint Green Sauce
Minted Yogurt Sauce
Mornay Sauce
Mousseline Sauce
Mushroom and Walnut Sauce
Mustard Sauce
Mustard Shallot Butter
Oriental Dressing
Pasta Pronto Sauce
Pineapple Marinade
Pistachio Butter Sauce
Poulette Sauce
Pumpkin Salsa
Raw Salsa
Red Pepper Sauce
Red Salsa

Remoulade Sauce
Roasted Red Pepper Salsa
Rouille
Russian Dressing
Saffron Sauce
Sauce Gribiche
Sauce Meunière
Sauce Nantua
Sesame Sauce
Shallot Butter
Shrimp Butter
Smoked Salmon Butter
Soubise Sauce
Sour Cream Sauce
South of the Border Mayonnaise
Sun-dried Tomato Mayonnaise
Swedish Mustard Sauce
Sweet Pepper Sauce
Sweet and Sour Sauce
Tangy Lime Salsa
Tapenade Mayonnaise
Tarragon Cream Sauce
Tartare Sauce
Teriyaki Grilling Sauce
Teriyaki Sauce
Thousand Island Dressing
Tomatillo Salsa
Tomato Basil Mayonnaise
Tomato Basil Sauce
Tomato Caper Sauce
Tomato Cream
Tomato Puree
Walnut Garlic Sauce
Walnut Mayonnaise
White Wine Marinade
Yogurt Dill Sauce
Yogurt Garlic Dressing
Yogurt Walnut Sauce

❦ SAUCES FOR FRUIT

Amaretto Cherry Sauce
Apricot Sauce
Blueberry Sauce
Cider Lemon Sauce
Cranberry Catsup
Cranberry Sauce
Fresh Strawberry Sauce
Gingered Pear Sauce
Melba Sauce
Orange Cream Sauce
Orange Sauce I and II
Peach Cream Sauce
Peach Sauce
Raspberry Sauce
Sweet Plum Sauce

❦ SAUCES FOR GAME

Apple Cream Sauce
Apple and Ginger Sauce
Basic Red Wine Sauce
Cranberry Catsup
Cumberland Sauce
Fresh Cherry Sauce
Game Marinade
Game Sauce
Muscovite Sauce
Orange Port Sauce
Pepper Sauce (Poivrade)
Port Wine Sauce
Raisin Sauce
Savory Black Currant Sauce
Smitane Sauce
Supreme Sauce

❦ SAUCES FOR GRILLED MEATS (BEEF, PORK, ETC.)

Anchovy Butter
Anchovy Sauce
Bercy Butter
Black Pepper Butter
Choron Sauce
Cold Mustard Sauce
Fresh Vegetable Sauce
Garlic Butter
Garlic and Honey Marinade
Gorgonzola Butter
Green Peppercorn Butter
Grill Sauce
Herb Butter
Honey Mustard Marinade
Marinara Sauce
Mustard Sauce
Peanut Sauce
Pumpkin Salsa
Quick Horseradish Sauce
Raw Salsa
Red Salsa
Savory Plum Sauce
Shallot Butter
Spicy Mustard Sauce
Sweet Red Pepper Sauce
Vegetable Mignonette Sauce
Yogurt Dill Sauce

❦ SAUCES FOR LAMB

Anchovy Mayonnaise
Apple Mayonnaise
Avgolemono

Blue Cheese Brandy Butter
Cold Curry Sauce
Creamy Curry Mayonnaise
Cucumber Sauce
Game Marinade
Garlic and Rosemary Marinade
Greek Tsatsiki
Lemon Barbecue Sauce
Lemon Marinade
Mignonette Sauce
Mint Green Sauce
Mint Sauce
Minted Yogurt Sauce
Peach Chutney
Roquefort Sauce
Rosemary Basting Sauce
Rosemary Sauce
Smitane Sauce
Stock-based Curry Sauce
Supreme Sauce
Yogurt Dill Sauce

❧ SAUCES FOR PASTA

Avocado Butter
Basil Sauce
Bolognese Sauce
Carbonara
Chicken Liver and Tomato Sauce
Classic Mushroom Sauce
Cognac Sauce
Easy Tomato Sauce
Eggplant Sauce
Farmhouse Spaghetti Sauce
Fra Diavolo
Fresh Tomato Sauce
Garlic Basil Butter

Goat Cheese Sauce
Ham and Walnut Sauce
Hazelnut Sauce
Herb Sauce
Hot Tomato Sauce
Leek and Tomato Sauce
Marinara Sauce
Mornay Sauce
Mushroom Cheese Sauce
Onion Pepper Sauce
Pasta Pronto Sauce
Pesto
Puttanesca Sauce
Red Pepper Sauce
Ricotta and Tomato Sauce
Rustic Tomato Sauce
Seafood Sauce
Smoked Salmon Sauce
Smoky Tomato Sauce
Spinach Sauce
Spring Vegetable Sauce
Sun-dried Tomato and Basil
    Butter
Three Cheese Sauce
Tomato Basil Sauce
Tomato Puree
Wild Mushroom Sauce
Yogurt and Prosciutto Sauce

❧ SAUCES FOR PORK

Aioli
Apple and Ginger Sauce
Apple Cream Sauce
Apple Mayonnaise
Bigarade
Brandied Marinade

Bread Sauce
Cranberry Catsup
Cranberry Salsa
Dijon Yogurt Dressing
Double Mustard Sauce
Espagnole Sauce
Fresh Cherry Sauce
Fresh Fruit Salsa
Fruity Marinade
Garlic and Honey Marinade
Ginger Glaze
Ginger Lime Mayonnaise
Ginger Sauce
Green Salsa
Honey Mustard Marinade
Lemon Barbecue Sauce
Maître d'Hôtel Butter
Old-fashioned Barbecue Sauce
Olive Salsa
Onion Pepper Sauce
Orange Port Sauce
Oriental Dressing
Oriental Orange Marinade
Peach Chutney
Peanut Sauce
Pico de Gallo
Pineapple Marinade
Pork Barbecue Sauce
Port Wine Sauce
Raisin Sauce
Ravigote Sauce (Hot)
Red Currant Glaze
Rib Sauce
Sate Sauce
Savory Black Currant Sauce
Savory Plum Sauce
Sicilian Sauce
Soubise Sauce
Soy Marinade
Sweet and Sour Sauce

❧ SAUCES FOR POULTRY

Almond Butter
Aurore Sauce
Avgolemono
Beurre Blanc
Bigarade
Blender Hollandaise
Brandied Marinade
Bread Sauce
Carlton Butter
Chipotle Sauce
Choron Sauce
Classic Mushroom Sauce
Cognac Sauce
Cold Curry Sauce
Cranberry Salsa
Cranberry Sauce
Creamy Curry Sauce
Curried Yogurt Sauce
Double Mustard Sauce
Easy Tomato Sauce
Fresh Cherry Sauce
Fresh Fruit Salsa
Garlic and Honey Marinade
Green Yogurt Sauce
Herb Sauce
Herb Butter
Honey Soy Basting Sauce
Lemon Barbecue Sauce
Lemon Mayonnaise
Lemon Mustard Sauce
Lemon Wine Sauce
Lime Basting Sauce
Lime and Pepper Butter
Louis Dressing
Mole Sauce
Mornay Sauce
Mushroom and Walnut Sauce

Mushroom Cheese Sauce
Old-fashioned Barbecue Sauce
Pasta Pronto Sauce
Peanut Sauce
Port Wine Sauce
Red Wine Marinade
Rosemary Basting Sauce
Savory Plum Sauce
Sesame Sauce
Shallot Butter
Soubise Sauce
South American Cheese Sauce
South of the Border Mayonnaise
Soy Marinade
Stock-based Curry Sauce
Supreme Sauce
Sweet Red Pepper Sauce
Tangy Lime Salsa
Tapenade Mayonnaise
Tarragon Cream Sauce
Teriyaki Sauce
Velouté
Walnut Mayonnaise
Wild Mushroom Sauce

SAUCES FOR SALADS

Apple Mayonnaise
Basil Mayonnaise
Basic Vinaigrette
Blue Cheese Dressing
Caesar Dressing
Caper Dressing
Cheddar Cheese Dressing
Chunky Red Pepper Vinaigrette
Classic Roquefort Dressing
Cold Curry Sauce
Coriander Vinaigrette
Creamy Italian
Creamy Jalapeño Dressing
Creamy Orange Dressing
Dijon Yogurt Dressing
Dill and Buttermilk Dressing
Ginger Lime Mayonnaise
Ginger Vinaigrette
Goat Cheese Dressing
Greek Cheese Dressing
Green Goddess Dressing
Green Vinaigrette
Guacamole Sauce
Hazelnut Dressing
Horseradish Dressing
Hot Bacon Dressing
Jalapeño Vinaigrette
Margarita Dressing
Middle Eastern Eggplant Sauce
Old-fashioned French Dressing
Onion Vinaigrette
Orange Yogurt Dressing
Oriental Dressing
Poppy Seed Dressing I, II, III
Provençal Dressing
Raspberry Dressing
Red Pepper Dressing
Russian Dressing
Sesame Seed Dressing
Spinach Dressing
Sun-dried Tomato Mayonnaise
Thousand Island Dressing
Thyme Dressing
Tomato Basil Mayonnaise
Watercress Dressing
Wine Vinaigrette
Yogurt Dill Sauce
Yogurt Walnut Sauce

❧ SAUCES FOR SHELLFISH

Aioli
Basil Mayonnaise
Beurre Blanc
Butter Herb Sauce
Cold Mustard Sauce
Creamy Curry Sauce
Creole Sauce
Fra Diavolo
Fresh Vegetable Salsa
Garlic Butter
Garlic Cream
Green Goddess Dressing
Green Mayonnaise
Hot Pepper Blender Hollandaise
Louis Dressing
Margarita Dressing
Marinara Sauce
Mignonette Sauce
Newburg Sauce
Olive Salsa
Onion Pepper Sauce
Parsley Sauce
Poulette Sauce
Remoulade Sauce
Russian Dressing
Saffron Sauce
Sauce Nantua
Shrimp Butter
Smoky Tomato Sauce
Snail Butter
Tarragon Cream Dressing
Thousand Island Dressing
Three Pepper Marinade
Tomato Cream
Vegetable Mignonette Sauce
Yogurt Walnut Sauce

❧ SAUCES FOR VEAL

Classic Mushroom Sauce
Cognac Sauce
Eggplant Sauce
Marinara Sauce
Mushroom and Walnut Sauce
Pasta Pronto Sauce
Roquefort Sauce
Sicilian Sauce
Tapenade Mayonnaise
Tuna Sauce
Wild Mushroom Sauce

❧ SAUCES FOR VEGETABLES

Aioli
Anchovy Mayonnaise
Avgolemono
Avocado Butter
Basil Mayonnaise
Beurre Blanc
Blender Hollandaise
Classic Hollandaise
Classic Mushroom Sauce
Classic Roquefort Dressing
Cold Mustard Sauce
Crab Sauce
Creamy Curry Sauce
Creamy Garlic Sauce
Creamy Mustard Sauce
Double Mustard Sauce
Garlic Butter
Garlic Sauce
Ginger Sauce
Gorgonzola Butter
Hazelnut Butter Sauce

Herbed Avocado Sauce
Hot Horseradish Sauce
Hot Pepper Blender Hollandaise
Lemon Cream Sauce
Lemon Mustard Sauce
Lime Butter
Lyonnaise Sauce
Maltaise Sauce
Mint Hollandaise
Mint Mayonnaise
Minted Yogurt Sauce
Mornay Sauce
Mousseline Sauce
Mushroom Cheese Sauce
Mustard Shallot Butter

Onion Béchamel
Pistachio Butter Sauce
Ravigote Sauce
Roquefort Sauce
Sesame Sauce
Shallot Butter
Snail Butter
Soubise Sauce
South American Cheese Sauce
Sun-dried Tomato and Basil Butter
Sun-dried Tomato Mayonnaise
Supreme Sauce
Tarragon Cream Dressing
Vegetable Marinade I and II
Yogurt Dill Sauce

❧ Index